Life, Death, and Community

in Cairo's City of the Dead

Hassan Ansah

iUniverse, Inc.
New York   Bloomington

Life, Death, and Community in Cairo's City of the Dead

iUniverse books may be ordered through booksellers or by contacting:

iUniverse
1663 Liberty Drive
Bloomington, IN 47403
www.iuniverse.com
1-800-Authors (1-800-288-4677)

ISBN: 978-1-4502-6700-7 (pbk)
ISBN: 978-1-4502-6701-4 (ebk)

Printed in the United States of America

iUniverse rev. date: 11/4/2010

Contents

Preface

Death is not the end, Death can never be the end. Death is a road, Life is the traveler, the Soul is the guide.
—Sri Chinmoy

In 2006 I was assigned to Cairo, Egypt as a Middle East correspondent for IRIN news agency, while there I also worked as a college lecturer on international relations at the American University of Cairo. During my tenure in Cairo I tried to assimilate and submerge myself as much as possible into Egyptian culture. When I wasn't teaching or writing, I spent the vast majority of my time wandering the diverse neighborhoods of Cairo, interacting with people from different levels of society, analyzing the city, and trying to interpret my observations with a cohesive logic. It was my first visit to the City of the Dead that I was able to really interact in a less formal sense with Cairo's so called marginalized populace. It was here in the cemeteries that my senses where awakened, my curiosity deepened, and my appreciation for Egyptian folk culture heightened.

The essence of the city of the dead comes alive with the rich stories of its citizens, the historical legacy in its architecture, and reconciling of the ordinary with the extraordinary and the profane with the sacred. This rich tapestry reflects a very little known alternative world view that weaves a complex and intricate web of symbols and half-hidden references which hangs at the very heart of the culture. There is a profound transformation that takes place when a veil is undraped from mundane lives and hidden emotions. Here in the cemeteries it seemed that everyone had an extraordinary story to tell.

When observing the people of this community getting together, it often seemed as if everyone would be talking at once, yet all ears are acutely tuned and aware of even the subtlest nuance within the divergent conversations. Although this book is listed under history, it actually defies categorization; a rich mixture of fable, folk tale, historic continuity, personal anecdote, and moral philosophy. I have set out to transport my readers into an exotic and hidden culture where fate seems to parallel reason and western logic. Ordinary people seem to suffer extraordinary challenges and tribulations, yet I experienced first hand a community of poor yet proud and resourceful people, who despite the odds, were eking out a legacy that could change the very face of their country. Here are the voices of a community both ancient and modern, religious and spiritual, hidden and scene, forever in between hope and despair, defeat and triumph, life and death. Welcome to Qarafa (the city of Cemeteries) and the remarkable municipality that lives amongst the dead.

Chapter 1
The Birth of Qarafa (The Cemeteries)

"Death is the golden key that opens the door to heaven's tomorrow to fresh woods and pastures new! It is natural to die- as to be born. Heaven gives its favorites an early death. If your riches are yours, why don't you take them to the other world?"
—Immortal Saying: Author unknown

Egypt has had an intimate relationship with the concept of death since time immemorial. The long tradition of a funerary culture, mythology, as well as the architecture of Pharaonic Egypt persisted throughout the Greek, Roman, and the Christian periods. Islamic Egypt would not be an exception, despite the Arab conquerors surface aversion to the ancient practices of the cult of the dead and to its physical locus, the cemeteries.

Sketchy estimates have the potential number of more than three million inhabitants living among this urban scuffle, garbage, and seemingly desperate stretch of chaos officially known as Qarafa (Arabic for Cemeteries), better known as the City of the Dead. For many Egyptians, the Cemeteries are a mysterious, foreboding, and even disdained area. The majority of citizens are only marginally aware of its existence, but even fewer understand the large historical relevance and complex culture that make up this group of vast cemeteries that stretch out along the base of the Moqattam Hills. In Cairo, often the closest that the residence come to ever seeing the cemeteries is by driving over it on the Salah Salim Highway. The majority of people who pass by this ancient burial community dare to even stop, let alone venture inside. From the vantage point of this elevated highway, the Cemeteries appear as an orderly and organized part of Cairo. It is truly possible to pass through these vast ancient necropolises and completely fail to recognize its unique and complex history and culture. Like most huge cities its size, Cairo suffers from a deep and chaotic lack of organized and affordable housing. Indeed this housing crises can be seen within much of the developing world, from Mexico City to Kolkata, India. With over twenty million people in this capital city, housing becomes a luxury rather than a right for the majority of its poor. Because its society can be so oppositional towards the lower classes, many inhabitants have resorted to survival techniques which are outside of the law in what many social theorists called the informal sector. This area consists of activities outside of the radar of the states official procedure policies. In fact one can say that the entire City of the Dead is an informal city. If one scratches the surface, its very easy to see that within these cemeteries resides a hidden, vibrant, and even cohesive dimension of Cairo's urban poor, forming a sometimes illegal, but often tolerated, separate society with its own culture, values, and traditions.

As I pass by the many tombs that have been converted into houses, I observed energetic children running around playing soccer between old decaying buildings and garbage-strewn streets. One of the most creative things that I noticed was the unique usage of wood coffins located inside these tomb/homes that would serve as everything from ironing boards to dinner tables, from benches to beds. One factor that often serves as a deterrent to outsiders, especially westerners, is the fact that the majority of the people living here are technically illegal squatters. In terms of the state policy, there is no sewer or trash servicing these parts. One's initial impression when entering the gates is that every street corner is heaved with garbage and many of the side alleys are running a sway with raw sewage.

The more deeply one penetrates these quarters, the more elusive the cultures continuity becomes.

There are five major cemeteries that build the foundation for what is collectively known as the City of the Dead: the Northern Cemetery, the Southern Cemetery, the Cemetery of the Great, and Bab el Wazir. The Northern Cemetery, which is the most famous, begins at the north – East corner of the Citadel and extends northwards into the Cairo suburb of Nasr City. The Salah Salim Highway runs along its border to the west, while the mystical Moquattam Hills flank the eastern half of the cemetery. The Southern Cemetery is on the other side of the highway, opposite the Cemetery of the Great. It expands from the Eastern side of the Citadel up to the modern upscale Cairo suburb of Maadi. It is boarded on one side by the highway and on the other side by sharp slopes of the Motquattam Hills.

The cemetery of the Great is south of Salah al-Din's majestic Citadel and lies mostly on the west side of the Salah Salim highway. Finally, across the huge highway from the Northern Cemetery lies the Bab al-Nasr Cemetery, which extends from the ancient Fatimid gate and wraps up around the front of Salah –al –Din's Citadel.

The Arab conquest: Qarafa came into conception parallel with the birth of the rest of Cairo. In the year 639 AD General Amr Ibn Al-As came to Egypt with his army there was no Cairo as we know it today. The ancient city of Heliopolis (On) was located on the east bank and the ancient capital of Memphis was located among the pyramids on the west bank of the Nile. After the defeat of the Roman army, the Arab conquerors set up their camp garrison city Fustat, the Entrenched Camp, just north of this area. An area in close proximity to the Muqattam Hills, north of today's Citadel, was chosen as the official cemetery covering a mass of over six kilometers. Ironically, the cemeteries actually existed years before the official birth of Cairo itself. It wasn't until 639 AD that it officially became Al-Qahira (the Victorious) the dynamic, vibrant, and sometimes overwhelming city that we all know today. The young religion of Islam, brought by general Amr Ibn, also swept through Cairo and eventually all of Egypt. The new Islamic inhabitants however had to adapt to an ancient cultural modality which was influenced by the oldest civilization in the world.

This cross section of cultural emersion was more apparent in certain aspects of social functioning, especially in regards to how the vast majority of Arab Muslims incorporated many of the ancient Pharaonic practices into there religious and social ceremonies, the most profound being the deep reverence for the after life and its numerous funerary practices.

Although there are no grand pyramids or majestic mummies that call on the ancient wisdom from the eternal afterlife, there can be found a plethora of architectural and indigenous customs that are traditionally linked to ancient Egypt. The conquering Arabs continued the practice of nurturing the dead as well as the tradition of building living spaces within the area of the deceased. The dead were often buried in partially hidden underground tombs, which could be re-opened for future burials. This allows different generations of the family to be entombed in the same burial space.

Another very ancient Egyptian cultural tradition is the aspect of building extra living quarters in order to house additional family members during the forty days mourning ceremony. Today this practice is not only found in communities such as the Cemeteries, but also in Upper Egypt where the native Nubians have practice this thousands of years before the advent of Islam. In more traditional customs of Islam, there is no crying during funeral processions. There should also be no wearing of black and absolutely no forty-day mourning period. These practices are seen as being contrary to the divine will of God. In Egypt, Islam adapted to the death cult traditions that date back to the ancient Pharaonic kings. For example, Egyptian Muslims still observe this forty-day mourning period, which derives from the length of time it took the ancient Pharaonic Priest to purify the body in order to preserve it as a Mummy.

The most ancient tombs can be found in the Southern Cemetery better known as" Al-Ashriffiyya" in Arabic or simply" the Cemetery of the Great." Ironically one of the most historic tombs found in this section of the Cemetery is that of Imam al-Shafi'I, which is the largest Islamic mortuary chamber in Egypt. This tomb surely illustrates a spiritual and historic foundation and articulates symbolically how the City of the Dead developed into its present day composition. Although Imam al-Shafi died in Egypt in 819 A.D, the presence of his tomb is only officially recorded from the year of 1210 A.D. It is covered with a very large copper dome, which can be seen from other points in Cairo. This actual dome was built in 1721 by the famous architect Ali Bey al- Kebir and is rumored to resemble the holy Dome of the Rock in Jerusalem.

Throughout the Sunni Muslim world, Imam al-Shafi'I is esteemed as one of the greatest of Muslim saints. His tomb attracts hundreds of

Muslim pilgrims looking to perform" ziyyarah" or the Islamic concept of making special prayer in his honor. From its very inception the cemeteries here have been destinations for the sick looking to be cured by the spiritual power of revered saints. Imam al –Shafii's tomb would be no exception to this rule. It is here that many Muslims come to find "BARAKA" or spiritual blessings.

The concept of BARAKA, which is a mystical Islamic symbolic act, is so essential to understanding this communities special relationships with its beloved saints. BARAKA can be translated as an effusion of blessing or spiritual grace from the deceased. Likened to the concept of Chi in the Chinese culture, or the Holy Spirit in the Christian world view.

In relation to the Qarafa, this religious act takes on the aspect of power emanating from relics taken from the vicinity of saints or holy graves to that of praesentia, or "the physical presence of the holy". The spiritual essence is thus not the holy per se but a force emanating from the sacred, or a physical reminder of it- blessing by association. Many writers even speak about a Pharaonic connection with the word and concept. For example in ancient Egyptian religion, the word BA was representative of person's soul, RA was considered the emanation of the creative force in the universe, while the KA was the soul's connection to the universal spirit. Again we can see the influence of ancient concepts consolidating with modern ones.

This leads us to the most important aspects between BARAKA and its relationship to the cemeteries. The Walis, or important Sufi Sheikhs buried in theses walls are renowned for carrying a very special type of BARAKA. Because of their pious nature and honorable deeds when alive, their graves are often perceived by many as a potential guide to Divine mercy in the afterlife. Many of the saint's graves are also seen as being able to mystically intervene with god on the supplicant's behalf.

The City of Dead became an extremely influential burial ground during the arrival of the Mamluks, (meaning the possessed in Arabic), around 1250 AD. They were slave soldiers from Turkey and the Black Sea area who were brought to Egypt as servants and raised under the control of the ruling Sultan (Islamic King). Once they matured, many where often freed and stayed in Egypt to help influence a very unique form of architecture, in which Today's City of Dead is probably the best place to witness its remains.

As we arrived at the City of the Dead, both my driver and the interpreter wanted to first show case the vast historical mosques which palpitate throughout cemeteries. I, however, was much more interested in meeting the everyday people that inhabit this city in order to get a first hand cultural perspective from its residence. Having grown up close to urban America, I've always had a strange and sincere affinity for those considered to be the outcasts of society, of low birth rank, and the marginalized of society.

Walking into the city's narrow and enigmatic dusty alleys, passing thru heaps of layered garbage, from which stray dogs feasted, initially felt no different than being in any other poor crowded section of Cairo. However, looking closer my eyes met a colorful tapestry of intricately interlocked buildings intermingled with historical monuments. Many of them separated by spacious streets in some areas and dusty narrow roads in others. In many areas the structures are neatly organized and arranged. In others the structures seem almost chaotic and lacking any semblance of cohesion.

Suddenly, I found myself in a beautiful large stone mausoleum directly connected to a living quarter. It was at this moment that I felt I was somewhere truly special. This Mausoleum was designed in beautiful white stone that was handsomely carved with sinewy Arabic script telling the story of who the deceased were. Many of these elaborate structures required guardians and /or caretakers to have built in housing accommodations. Ironically the tomb care takers and their families formed the first communities of the City of Dead.

Standing at the entrance of this huge building was a middle aged dark skinned woman wearing a clean black Galbiyya (a traditional Arabic dress). I greeted her in my very limited Arabic with salem alyekum" (How are you in Arabic), in which she gave a knowing smile that I was not a local. Sensing my obvious curiosity she motioned me to come inside. My interpreter went in first in order to initiate the conversation in Arabic.

She said that her name was Niriman Ali and that she was a fifty year old widow who was born in the Qarafa (the cemeteries). She has four children, two girls and two boys, whom she practically raised on her own since being widowed at a very early age. I asked her if this is where she and her family lived. She said no, that she simply worked on these grounds watching over and maintaining the two large marbled tomb stones. She went on to explain the differences between the two primary types of tombs found here. These large, beautifully designed, and elaborately put together tombs belonged to Cairo's wealthy families, many existing here for hundreds of years, always being attended to by the locals.

She pointed out a narrow pathway leading into an open space which was much less aesthetically pleasing. It was here that she pointed in the direction of two badly painted wooden tombs. These tombs belong to Cairo's poor and reflect how the vast majority of Egyptians living and dying in Qarafa will be buried. I ask my interpreter if this is where her family lay to rest. She smiled and shyly nodded her head signaling that it was. Ironically this was also where her family lived.

She led us farther down a dirt path, a cenotaph (Islamic tomb) that was still partially under construction. A narrow set of steps ascending led to an even smaller opening, and then down, perhaps eight to ten feet, was the burial chamber beneath. Two empty tiled chambers were square-seven by seven feet and they were covered with oddly curved roofs.. Nirman explained to us the that the men of the family are buried in the left-hand chamber, the women in the right. Bodies are not clothed. When another member of the family dies, the limestone floor is then reopened and the additional body is added. Up to twenty –five of each gender will fill a tomb this size.

Often times the dead are buried in underground tombs that are dug directly beneath the family's room or in the courtyards. As a foreigner it was fascinating to observe that many of Egypt's social stratifications: separation of the sexes as well as its rigid social classism would be so strictly adhered to even after the process of death.

Unlike most western graves, the underground cavities can be either large or small, depending on the wealth of the family and will often times have a single entrance and the door of the tomb is typically covered by a few rocks and a thin layer of dirt. If one removes the rocks and dirt you can see a narrow dark stair way leading down into the burial chamber.

To the un initiated eye, the door to the tomb was not very conspicuous, yet its discernable for the family members and caretakers who live here. Once again we confront the contradiction of cultures that is so pervasive here in the cemeteries. The traditional process of having a Muslim funeral here involves the initial rites of cleaning the body while the Koran is being recited. this is the first step in the actual burial process. The body is wrapped in white cloth and transferred into the single door opening of the burial chamber. The walls of the tomb will be painted in lime and mixed with henna in order to absorb the added moisture with the burial chamber. The use of henna actually pre- dates the Islamic invasion. The ancient Egyptians believed that placing henna under the deceased would help to facilitate the soul's journey into the afterlife. In modern Islamic tradition the corpse is then brought into the actual tomb and the head lays facing Mecca hoping to insure the soul's entrance into Paradise.

This process helps to keep the dynamic of the community going here because the dead are often visited by family members during their birthdays, family feast, and particularly during religious festivals such as Ramadan. As previously stated, the traditional Egyptian attitude toward cemeteries and the dead in general differed greatly from the conventional Islamic perception of them. Throughout time ancient Egyptians refuse to see the process of death as a dark, evil, or even a remorseful process. Here in Cairo's City of the Dead these holistic and encompassing views of the cemetery are still an active and intricate part of the living community.

As we left the compound and entered the outside yard, my eyes immediately are drawn to a very attractive, brown skinned, statuesque lady wearing a black velour galabiyya and higab (Traditional Islamic head covering) who was intently focused on watering what seemed to be very dry and anemic looking aloe plants that were growing in the vicinity of the tombs. The lady was her eldest daughter Aiza Saad Brahim. I ask my interpreter if there was any significance of her watering the plants so close to the tombs? Niriman enthusiastically explained that these particular plants played a very significant role in Islamic burial grounds, they where symbolic of the qualities representative of what good Muslims should practice in the face of death: endurance, patience, and faithfulness. She then said that the dead must also drink, "**The hospitality of the desert sanctions that one must always provide water to those in need**!

Niriman and her daughter offered tea as we where joined by her grand children who although curious about foreigners, kept a respectful distance. As I drank the tea I looked and searched for answers in my head as to how three generations continue to exist in such a place without making progress? Than I considered that maybe their concept of progress was much different then my own.

We ask Niriman if she has ever considered moving herself and her family out of the cemeteries. Her expression became very pensive and serious and she said that she would love to move her family to a more affluent area of Cairo, but lack of money and a chronic housing shortage makes it virtually impossible. The other thing that keeps her here is the opinion that the residents are more generous, kinder and warmer then in any other part of Cairo. We thanked her for her warm hospitality and openness and told her that we wish the best for her and her family in the future. She smiled and stated" Inshallah" (God willing).

Chapter 2
The rule of The Fatimids and the rise of Islamic mysticism

"Death is but a changing of our robes to wait in wedding garments at the Eternal's gate."
—Sri Aurobindo

In 969 AD, when Fatimid Caliph al-Mu'izz li-Din Allah sent an army into Egypt under the command of General Gawhar al –Siqilly with only 100,000 soldiers he met little resistance from the residence of al-Fustat (the Arab name for the original capital). Unlike the previous rulers, the fatimids were Shi'I Muslims, which means that they claim decent from the Prophet through his daughter Fatima and hereditary succession through Ali, his successor. This religious rift is still playing out today in places such as Iraq, Lebanon, and Iran. During this time of great prosperity the majority of Egyptians, (who are Sunni Muslims), were very open towards Shi'I rule. The Fatimids continued to use the cemetery as their primary burial ground, they extended the cemetery to the Northeast, and built much of the mausoleum that today constitute the Southern Cemetery. They also constructed shrines, mosques, shrines, and even residences inside the burial places and increased the integration of the cemeteries as an active part of the living community, not simply as a resting ground for the deceased.

Situated deep within the fringes of the Southern Cemetery is buried one of the most interesting and mysterious figures within the world of Islamic spirituality Dhul-Nun al-Misri. Born to Nubian parents in the ancient Egyptian city of Akhmin in Upper Egypt, he is known as the father of Sufism (the mystical branch of Islam). While many of the factual events in his life are often clouded in idealistic fiction, there are enough historical details to gain a tangible grasp of his legacy and the influence that his thoughts and writings have had, not only on Egypt, but throughout the Islamic world. He studied under numerous teachers and although he spent the majority of his life in Cairo, Dhul-Nun traveled extensively throughout the Middle East and Africa. His poems and wise quotations are extremely rich and intricate with Sufi symbolism that place a heavy emphasis on knowledge or gnosis (m'arifah) over fear (makhafah) or love (mahabbah), the other two paths of spiritual enlightenment within Sufism.

As a legendary alchemist and linguist he supposedly knew the secret of Egyptian hieroglyphics long before the Rosetta stone was discovered. None of his actual written work has survived, however a vast collection of poems, sayings, and aphorisms attributed to him continues to survive in the form of oral folklore. His sayings gave birth to such a depth and a sophistication of aesthetic profundity and theoretical speculation that he is often said to have influenced the entire foundation of later works of Sufi giants such as Rumi and Omar Katayam. He was a master of the epigram and a polished poetic stylist in Arabic. The true depth and intensity of his literary talent comes to light in his prayers.

"True knowledge of god is not the knowledge that god is one, which is possessed by all believers, nor the knowledge of him derived from proof and demonstration, which belongs to philosophers, rhetoricians, and theologians, but it is the knowledge of the attributes of divine unity, which belongs to the saints of god, those who behold god with their hearts in such ways that he reveals unto them what he revealeth not unto anyone else in the world." (D'hul- Nun)

During one of Dhu'l Nun travels in Baghdad, he was imprisoned by the caliph al-Mutawakkil because of his refusal to accept the Caliph's doctrine of the divine infallibility of the Koran. For this refusal he received a life sentence. During the trial, however his profundity of thought and mystical insight so impressed al-Mutawakkil, that the caliph released him. He was one the first founders of the comprehensive theory of the conjunction of opposites. Ma'rifah, (spiritual gnosis), which completely contrast with the more conservative and traditional path of discursive reasoning so often found in more popular versions of Islamic thought. A key and root aspect of Dhu'l –Nun's visionary philosophy within unity within diversity. Legend has it that during his death the following statement was uttered before his last breath. "This is the beloved of God, who died in God's love. **"This is the slain of God, who died by God's sword". (Dhul-Nun)**

Somewhat removed from the main area of the Southern Cemetery and elevated by the mythically rich Moquattam Hills, stands the mosque and mausoleum of Amr al-Guyushi. He was a famous Fatimid minister who ruled Egypt for two decades. The actual mosque dates from 1085 A.D. and commands a magnificent view of Cairo. Although it's not known who is buried in the actual shrine, the building is a stunning example of early Fatimid architecture. It is constructed in typical Fatimid style: a square tower with a smaller square placed on top and covered by a gold dome. The minaret over the huge primary entrance is thought to be the oldest surviving minaret (tower), in Cairo.

Also Located in the same area is the tomb of one of the most beloved shrines within the City of the Dead, that of Syyida Nafisa. She was the actual granddaughter of Al- Hassan, the grandson of the prophet Muhammad. She traveled to Egypt during the during the later part of the seventh century and lived in a house in the same area as her present day tomb. The rumor is that she had felt death coming down upon her so she dug her own grave and piously prayed there until her death in 824 A.D. Amazingly much activity still takes place by it. I was informed that typically over a hundred marriages are performed there each week in order to ensure that the couples receive her **BARAKA** and allow their marriages to be strong and long-lasting.

There is a very important saying in Islamic Sufism," **if you want to know the Sharaf of the land (how honorable the land is), look to those buried in it"! Unknown Author.**

Most westerns who are interested in Sufism are usually familiar with a particular type of dancer named the Whirling Dervish.. Many outsiders who've witnessed this dance don't truly understand or appreciate the deeper esoteric meaning behind it. This actual style is a creation of the ancient Sufi sects that go back 700 years or possibly earlier. The world Sufi in Arabic means "wool" and it was a referral to the wool worn by its members who often lived an ascetic and nomadic lifestyle. Others contend the word Sufism derives from the Greek root word "Sophos", which means wisdom in Greek. After speaking to several experts on the subject, I was more convinced of the Greek origin of the word, which inevitably link one back to the very cultural essence of Sufism which many believe originated with Pharaonic mysticism, veiling itself under the guise of being a branch of Islam in order to protect its early members from religious persecution.

The history of the word Dervish however can be translated from the Persian meaning "standing on the still of the door", a symbolic reference to the door of enlightenment in which all Sufis seek. In western terms they can be compared to cross cultured Christian monks. Although the majority of dancers that perform on cruise boats and other large entertainment venues are not true practicing Sufis, but rather entertainers for tourists. On the edges of the City of the Dead can be found a traditional Dervish Sufi Theatre, here one can watch a live historically authentic whirling dervish performance.

It was a very windy day with a strange somewhat arcane filled aura when I decided to visit this Theater. A short Taxi ride takes one pass the Salah AD Din Citadel and the great mosque of Sultan Hassan, driving through the narrow streets of old Cairo I found the theatre across from a huge Qubba (dome) building. The building itself speaks not only to the ancient history of Egypt, but also to the complex cultural intermingling that has taken place throughout the Middle East. It was once part of the Mawali Sufi complex which once stood in this area. The term"Mawali", is Arabic for Teacher or Master.

Ironically this sect of Sufi dancing originated in Konya, Turkey, and was made by famous Sufi Poet Jalalud'dan El Rumi, who is one of the most widely read poets in the world. As specific Sufi ideas spread over most of Egypt, the Mawali settled in an area between the cemeteries and the Citadel. Constructing a massively beautiful complex with the entrance on Suffia Street close to the Northern Cemetery. This huge

Sufi complex was constructed during the 19th century, the more sacred parts actually being much older.

Upon entering into the complex, if feels as if one is transported into a truly sacred space. Is almost as if one walks through a vortex of time, or at the very least of culture. The loud, chaotic and seemingly endless noise of Cairo comes to a complete stop as one enters the theatre, leaving one with a tremendous sense of peace and cohesiveness within. On this particular evening there were thirteen other foreign spectators there to enjoy the festival. The actual theatre is a huge circular hall with walls that are covered with dark brown wood and intricately designed windows that allow specific amounts of light to come through at a certain angle in order to create an even more mystical aura. A very unique chandelier hangs distinctly over the large center stage.

The large gold Qubba ceiling is the most beautiful part of the theatre. It was built as a representation of the sky. When they perform their dance, this uniquely built ceiling becomes reflective of the opening of heavens gates and creates an atmosphere in which the dancers seem to merge with the universe. Beautiful gold plated verses taken from the Quran radiate a bright crimson color that is representative of the sun. Eloquent paintings of little birds painted throughout the ceiling symbolize the actual dancers who ponder the oneness of god and reflects the souls desire to be free.

Sitting across the room was an old man with a grey beard, piercing green eyes, and a long, white traditional galabeya (Islamic robe for men). With his warm smile he kept looking over at my interpreter and I. As I return his glance he finally gestured for us to come closer. After living in Egypt for over a year, I was now a little skeptical about starting up conversations with strangers knowing if often times it meant being asked for money or some other monetary good. There was a sincerity in his eyes that made me drop my natural skepticism and freely approach him. To my surprise his spoken English was very lucid. He introduced himself as Abdul and asked us if we had come to watch the Sufi dancers? I stated" yes of course", and we both started laughing. It turned out that Mr. Abdul was very informative and a bit of an self taught historian. He mentioned that the theatre was used by the Sufis not just to dance, but in order to perform specific rituals perceived as helping them become closer to God. He said that every movement involved with the dancers was a sacred act with the intention of getting beyond the human ego into a spiritual realm.

The dancing Dervishes wear black robes to symbolize the grave and long rigid camel hair hats to represent the actual headstones. These particular Sufis that now sport multi colored robes unique to Egyptian Sufism, believed that the world began at a point and ends at the same point. The Dervish gather in a circle in the center of the stage and then slowly, deliberately, and harmoniously rise up and move with the ritual music. They begin by greeting the leader of the group, as they slowly dance in circles which accelerate at a very fast pace.

Many of the delicate movements are conceptions of the satirical imaginations of a particular leader of the dance quartet. At times it seems a little disordered, however they are entrusted with centuries of accumulated wisdom and knowledge deliberated in moves created simply in the service of a spiritual ideal to be realized.

After the initial movements the dancers then cast off the multi colored robes that represents the tomb, therefore discarding all worldly attachments. They spin their left arms toward the floor and

their right arm is extended toward the sky becoming symbolic of heaven. With this act the dancers believe that grace is received from God and distributed to humanity. The Sufi dancers themselves are said to represent the actual celestial bodies circling the sun, represented by their sheikh and spiritual leader. A visitor can easily become transfixed and almost outright hypnotized by the splendid and delicate array of elaborate movements and perfect timing of the dancers. What started out as a strata of something oppressively solid was then revealed to be naught but an explosion of boundaries. The mystery of how it happens, the illusion that must sustain us, resides in the movements. Thus this art out of nothing, dancing for centuries in defiance of the ordinary, dares to triumph over disintegration. The mysterious Mr. Abdul then got up with out saying a word and simply disappeared into the dark hallway without asking for anything.

Now that the dance was over we got up and looked more closely at the actual theatre. On the first level there is an audience section for people to gather around the dancing dervishes and watch them while they perform their rituals. Unlike many of the tourist shows, there are no seats as the audience simply gathers around the circular stage where wooden pass way of stairs leads up to the second floor.

The second floor consists of three primary parts. The first is built like the lower floor which is simply a section to sit and watch the performances. The second section is ironically named the Harem section, which was created exclusively for female members of the audience. This section is covered with large dark wooden screens so that women can view the performance anonymously. Next to the women's section is the orchestra area, which has two small entrance ways that allow the musicians to enter. There is also a very delicately designed opening that is cut and measured with just enough precision that it enables the music to fill the entire building.

Beneath the actual theatre is a small museum which is now being refurbished, therefore we weren't allowed to enter. Like most things in or close to the City of the Dead, the Dervish Theatre is not part of the mainstream Egyptian tourist sites, but it is well worth visiting.

Chapter 3
Fridays market place in the City of the Dead

"The call of death is a call of love. Death can sweet if
we answer it in the affirmative, if we accept it as one of
the great eternal forms of life and transformation".
—Herman Hesse

For the average person visiting a foreign country thoughts of having a jubilee market festival in a place as solemn and foreboding as a Cemetery seems a little illogical, to say the least. Once again the duality of Egypt is found alive and well and seemingly functioning with its own logic. One of the primary sources are sustenance for the majority of citizens living here is the Suq al guma'a or Friday Market. Shopping at this Market within cemeteries is a very popular event that actually draws hundreds of Cairo's underserved every week to a place where they can both buy and sell goods at a price which is affordable to all. Every now and again the curious, adventurous, western tourists peak in to assess the potential value found amongst the seemingly piled up chaos within the crowds.

As I step outside of the Taxi I find myself standing directly in front of an energetic and almost frenzied crowed. Here in Egypt, frenzy is a relative term especially in the eyes of a native. Most westerns would recoil at the thought of buying clothing that had been worn by a dead person. Initially I was recoiled by the entire idea!. After several tangible experiences with such off putting concepts, its amazing how many western sensibilities begin to be challenged when intermingling with a culture that is so intimate with the other side, the world of the deceased, and the spiritual world of the unknown. Visiting the Friday market one's senses are surely expanded and challenged. There is almost a palpable sense of anticipation.

As we move closer into the center of the market, the crowd becomes so thick that we are pushed completely against our will in every direction except the one that we want to go in. The best bet for any sense of coherence was to stop off near a local vender and try to start a conversation. This allows us to momentarily sidestep this tempest of mass chaos in order to regain some semblance of direction. My interpreter and I both greet an old female vender with the traditional Saluu malakuum. She answers back wal lakuum Salaam, a common greeting that means peace be with you. We look over at the what she has stored in one stall and found pieces of a broken computer, coils of wire, used ladies and men's clothing, all for a price that anyone can afford. We both smiled and asked her the cost of a very uniquely made dressed. She looked, smiled, and then shouted out $100 pounds!!! I looked at Said and wondered why its was so expensive, he laughed at me and then mentioned that its customary for the people here to start their prices out by first sizing up buyers visually. If one looks as if he has money, is well dressed, or speaks with a foreign accent (i.e.: American or European), prices will commence very high.

As we continued down a narrow road we ran into a small man dressed in the typical white Islamic outfit and radiating a calm and honest demeanor. There was a new looking VCR lying beneath his selling stall. I told my interpreter to try and see what his asking price was? He looks around and then picks up a VRC, exclaiming that it's a Sony, a high quality machine made in Japan. I knew that was a code word for a high price. He looks very pensive and states that he could let the machine go for 80 Egyptian pounds, which compared to other parts of Cairo was a steal. Negotiation in Arabic may eventually get the VCR down to 40 pounds, (less than eight US dollars). There was a method to this madness, and real bargains could be had here, even for Americans like myself that speak very little Arabic.

As we move more adjacent into the marketplace, I am shocked to see such high a number of wild animals being sold. These are not simply domestic cats or dogs, but many more exotic animals such as monkeys, foxes, hawks, and even cobras.

I was very intrigued with a group of young men holding a sign in

Arabic claiming to sell cobras. From my earliest childhood memories I was always infatuated with snakes, and this was the Egyptian Cobra one of the most royal representations of it. Here was the famous mythological reptile that ended the life of the well known queen Cleopatra. Since my early childhood I could recall turning on the television and watching the snake charmers of Egypt seduce and completely render this very venomous creature harmless simply by the sound of a flute. I am sure that this image is still very popular. However the reality of snake charming is a little less romantic and anti dramatic. The majority of these snakes are de- venomized from an early age so the actual perceived danger is deceptive. After inquiring about how much the cost was for someone looking to purchase the cobra, the vender actually let me hold it. I smiled and stated that I wanted to first observe him picking up the snake. After seeing how non-aggressive it was, I cautiously attempted to handle the serpent myself and was presently surprised at how smooth and dry it felt.

As I looked around I was amazed to see caged falcons, hawks, jackals, monkeys, and even exotic turtles. One has to wonder where in the world these animals are being shipped too. Unlike the west, Egyptian culture is does not embrace pets as family companions. Even dogs and cats are often given the cold shoulder, let alone wild monkeys, hawks, or a vultures !

One can actually smell the animal sector blocks before you arrive. As I left the reptile section, I wandered into the bird of prey area. Here I observed a beautiful falcon and was curious to know what it ate. The vendor answered everything; chicken, beef, fish, even vegetables. I joke with him and stated," but no pork??" He half heartedly smiled and then began to chase away the young children that were busy teasing some of the animals.

As we headed further north away from the heart of the market and deeper into the actual cemetery, the animal market dwindles down to the last sparse chicken vendors. On the left sits a ram shackled clothing market where one can observe sellers laying their used clothing into large mounds within metal tarps. Crowds of people dig through them indiscriminately, holding up everything from socks, underwear, shirts, ties, and even used shoes. Meanwhile off to the left, a small funeral procession buzzes in and out of view through successive narrow alleyways, briefly reminding one of the mortuary celebrations that take place in New Orleans. Ironically in the City of Dead funerals are often speedy processes since Islamic custom requires burial before sunset on the day of death. Leading the procession was a pensive looking Koran reader wearing a dark blue kaftan (scarf) and a square, red-tasseled fez. I assumed that he was deeply contemplating what was to be said about the deceased as well as how to open up communication to the angels. As the caravan moves past us I notice how small it is: this dead man was probably not very well known nor wealthy.

moving southwards we come into a side street known as The Coin Seller's Alley. As we approach closer there is a loud man with brown teeth wearing a long grey turban doing the arduous process of asking people if they are interested in finding a specific type of coin? I was told by my interpreter that these are the most sophisticated and worldly venders within the Cemeteries. Speaking broken English with a very heavy Egyptian accent, the vender asked us if we would like to view old coins? Purchasing old Roman, Greek, Ottoman, and Coptic coins one has to be very careful, as seventy percent are not authentic and those that are have probably been pilfered illegally from archeological sites. I wouldn't recommend purchasing these coins if one isn't a professional coin dealer. Many have learned the hard way, and if you're truly unable to differentiate authentic coins from counterfeit ones, you're liable to purchase smelted down bronze junk. Since any type of trafficking in illegal artifacts carries a heavy jail sentence in Egypt, purchasing should be avoided.

I ask the vendor what kind of old coins is he selling today? The seller pulls out a huge white looking bowl from behind his stall, and very cautiously looks around as if not to alert the undercover police, empties a handful of copper and gold Ottoman and Greek coins. He also states that any special request such as Byzantine or Mamluk (ancient Turks) coins, or for the right price something more valuable than coins. I politely declined and we headed further south. We then pass by one of the strangest areas within the entire Cemetery: : The dog mating market. Like the very famous camel markets that are pervasive throughout much of Egypt, this spectacle is just as intense and the buyers are very as serious. People from all over Cairo would bring dogs of all shapes and sizes to negotiate a mating fee. The stronger looking dogs will of course attract the highest prices. Like most things in the city of the dead, time is of the essence.

Once a bargained fee is agreed upon, the people form a closed circle and watch as two dogs attempt to procreate. As you can imagine this often creates very humorous show. As I muscled my way inside of the circle, I was amused at the bewildered look as one male dog refused interest with an in heat female. My interpreter laughed and said maybe the dog is interested in the same sex. Other dog venders carry around small puppies, obviously the result of previous mating sessions which went a little more successfully than the one I witnessed. Since the majority of these canines end up on large farms out in villages in Upper Egypt, I am told that many of the buyers have actually traveled a day's time simply to come purchase one of these highly priced home bred farm dogs. Moving farther away from the crowd the market begins to thin out. From this point I observed the huge highway which was arranged to go over the cemeteries instead of through it. From here one can view one of the most beautiful parks in all of Cairo, the Al Azhar.

It sits overlooking the city of the dead like a huge class divider reflecting the great duality that so defines Egypt. Although many people would describe Cairo, if not all of Egypt, as being culturally circumscribed in irony, it was here in the City of the Dead that I truly tasted its essence and observed its biting ramifications.

As the crisp chill of nightfall began to creep over into the day and the market place abated down, my driver thought it would be wise if we began to close out the days tour and head home. I thought about recent studies suggesting that the population here is growing rapidly because of rural migration and Cairo's complex and congested housing crises that is often ignored. In my heart I felt a genuine admiration for the adaptive and inventive survival skills of these residence who have adjusted to this mysterious and somewhat scary land. These brave inhabitants live by the historic belief that the cemeteries are an active part of the community and not exclusively for the dead, but rather a place where life and death collide and fuse. What better place to observe this than in its Market.

Chapter 4
From slave to queen: The first and only female Sultana to Rule

"Death is the mother of beauty, hence from her alone shall come fulfillment to our dreams and our desires".
—Wallace Stevens.

The Mamluks seized control of Egypt in 1250 A.D. and extended the City of the Dead tremendously, building some of the most renowned monuments in its history. Not only did they add on to the existing monasteries and homes, but they created trading and sporting venues within the cemeteries.

The Mamluks, coming from the Arabic word meaning" owned", were a non-Arab mostly Turkish or Kurdish slaves owned primarily by persons who themselves had once been slaves. After being purchased in the servant markets as young boys, they were bought up in separate barracks in Greek spartan fashion, their education consisting primarily of military training. At puberty the majority of the these boys were released from slavery and then admitted into the service of their Amir or commander, who was very often their former owner. They even helped to perpetuate this system by buying their own young slaves to mold.

Thus unfolds one of the most fascinating periods of the City of Dead, if not Egypt itself "in which the Mamluk sultans governed Egypt for nearly three hundred years. With this governance emerges one of the most fascinating rulers in Cairo's history: Shajrat al-Durr (Tree of Pearls) the only woman sultana in all Islamic history and the first to rule Egypt since Cleopatra.

Shajar al-Durr was born in Armenia and became a slave in the harem of the Caliph Al-Mustapha Sim in Baghdad, (modern day Iraq). As a women of exceptional beauty, it wasn't long before the Caliph became enamored with Shajar's exotic charm and beauty and hence she became his favored wife. Since she would often get information that most women of her day would never be privy too, the Caliph was actually becoming more dependent on her insight, judgment, and decisions. She became the so called power behind the throne.

In 1249 the Caliph died from Cancer and tuberculosis. With a perfect sense of timing and a ruthless pragmatism, Shajar al-Durr did the unthinkable for a women in any Islamic society: she actually seized control of the post and hence taking control of all Egypt. At the time, Turan Shah, the caliphs eldest son, was far away serving as viceroy in Mesopotamia. Egypt itself was at war with Europe during the seventh Crusade. Knowing full well that if the army learned of its leader's death they could become unfocused, and perhaps even allow the infidels to conquer the Citadel. Shajar, along with her chief eunuch slave, circulated the lie that the Caliph was simply ill. Offerings were still brought in every day for the him, while Shajar kept up the masquerade and deception.

It took tens months for the caliphs son to return to Egypt, during which time She had kept the country together. Upon his return, the French had been defeated, and King Louis had been captured. The Caliphs son, showed gratitude towards those who kept his father's kingdom together and hence insured his ascent to power. Instead of being grateful and acknowledging their loyalty and competence, he instead granted his Arab friends in Mesopotamia, (modern day Iraq) positions of power. Needless to say, these actions offended the Mamluks who were the proudest and most competent army unit that Egypt had during this time. He in turn answered their protest with drunken threats and curses. He also threatened Shajar, whom he accused of withholding his father's riches and power from him. She immediately appealed to her Mamluk soldiers for help. As the they were already offended and disgruntled by the new Caliphs obvious disregard for their honor, dedication, and loyalty, they agreed to help her. On May 3, 1250, as Turan was leaving a feast in his honor, Baibar, a ruthless and dedicated Mamluk assassin, led a ban of soldiers towards Turan and mortally wounded him. Turan managed to escape temporarily but was eventually met with a barrage of arrows and he fell down and was finished off by a saber (a huge sword).

Despite her somewhat vulnerable and precarious situation, Shagar al Durr had successfully carried out the only coup d'etat by a woman in Islamic history. For eighty days she ruled as sultana. Once the ruling Sultan in Bagdad stated that the prophet Mohammed says, "Woe until nations governed by women"! He then declared that he would come to Egypt himself and bring a man to take over the reign of power. She soon got wind of this and being a strategic ruler decided to simply legitimize her rule by marrying her husband's chief Mamluk and naming him as the new sultan. Still planning to continue her influence behind the scenes, she persuaded him to divorce his wife allowing her to remain the only power behind the thrown.

For the time being, Shajar al Durr secured her legitimacy within the halls of power, but one day she found out about her husband's plan to take a Turkish princess as a second wife. The thought of being outmaneuvered by a former slave soldier and being jealous by nature drove her to extreme anger. With the perceived threat to the both here ego and power base, she was consumed with revenge.

Shajar summoned her rather submissive husband to the citadel. Upon entering the citadel he was stabbed to death by five assassins at her request. The myth is that after the killing she realized her fate was sealed for the worst. Horrified, the guilt -ridden queen tried in vain to spread a rumor that her husband had died a natural death, but eventually the truth leaked out and with it the lost of many vital allies that were key to her rise to power. She was eventually imprisoned within the Citadel with the same jewels that she supposedly ground to dust with a mortar. when her husband's son by his first wife was appointed as the next sultan, he delivered Shajar to the slave women of his mother. This slave woman proceeded to insult her and finally to bludgeon her to death with wooden shoes. She was then dragged naked by her feet and thrown from the top of the moat naked, with only a red silk colored garment around her waist. Some loyal supporters actually collected the remains of the former sultana and buried them in a small mausoleum that she had built earlier for herself here in the cemeteries. The tomb of shajar al-Durr still stands today as a beautiful mosaic in fine cut glass that indicates the direction of Mecca. In poetic symbolism dedicated to her, whose name in Arabic means Tree of Pearls, sits a tree bearing fruit formed by small pieces of mother of pearl. The copper cenotaph close by aptly reads:

"O ye stand beside my grave, show not surprise at my condition. Yesterday I was you. Tomorrow you will be as me."

Her tomb stands as a testament to the life of the Islamic world's first and last Sultana, a slave woman who managed to become a queen!

Chapter 5
Why we choose to live in the City of the Dead: Interviews with Its Residence

"A good name is better than precious ointment, and the day of death than the day of one's birth. Better is the end of a thing than the beginning there of"
—Ecclesiastes 7

After interviewing a family of women I was curious to know what are the effects of living in the cemeteries had on the men that lived there. One gentlemen that I spoke with gave me some insight on this. He stated that the majority of men who live in the City of Dead are perceived as failures for having to resort to a life in the cemeteries at all. The overriding perception is that they have failed as fathers and husbands for not being able to provide a safe and standard foundation of living for their families. For the vast majority of men, these thoughts weigh heavily on their minds both day and night. In Cairo one's social standing is peerless.

Interview with Mr. Rasheed Hussien: Mr. Hussien favorite attire seems to be Nike sports wear. At first glance, one would hardly expect that he was be a resident of the Qarafa. He however has not only lived here for the majority of his life, but was born in the Cemeteries. He states" My family comes from a small village outside of the Delta region in Lower Egypt. My parents thought that we would have better opportunities living in such close proximity to the center of Cairo. They also moved to this area because they would be closer to family and friends who migrated from our village. In fact there was a growing number of migrants from my family's village in the Delta resettling in the City of Dead. So, together my family set off to find a more prosperous life than the village could provide."

His family settled in a building built in the urbanized area close to the complex of the Sultan Qaybay in the Northern Cemetery. Although located directly in the middle of the cemetery their home doesn't contain a tomb. Here his father worked as a carpenter, and his mother stayed home in the typical Egyptian fashion to raise he and his five siblings.

Rasheed states," I grew up with very unusual opportunities, from a very young age I was recognized, at first by family members and then by people within the extended community, as being exceptionally intelligent. My parents did everything possible to ensure that I would have a formal education. Until I became older I didn't realize to what extent they had to sacrifice for me to get an education. My family would sometimes go without running water or electricity for a month in order pay for my school fees. I finished my education after secondary school and decided that I would become a teacher in Egypt's public school system. Although this may seem like a small accomplishment for some, for my family becoming a teacher was actually a huge achievement.

Shortly after the death of his father, Rasheed was faced with new and more complex problems. After the death of my father I had to take full responsibility of the small family business that my father spent most of his adult life trying to build. It was my education and experience that helped me to organize and understand how to run the family business. The carpeting business had actually proven to be more profitable than my teaching, and I found myself taking care of many neighborhood and community families. I am particularly busy during holidays, such as Ramadan, when the majority of the residents will save money in order to make some type of furnishing within their living space, regardless of small it may be. The same occurrence happens during other religious days in which times I can work up to 1 am in the morning.

Our everyday life is fairly comfortable in comparison to the average person who resides in the surrounding area. We have running water, electricity, and even a small television. The majority of people have to use the government-installed public telephones near the Mosque of Sultan Barquq. The average household also doesn't have running water but instead relies on the public tap water besides the huge Mosque near the center of our community.

As we walk with Rasheed down the dusty streets of this crowed section of Qarafa, its very obvious to see how highly regarded and respected he within his own community. Ironically when speaking he often seems to set himself apart from the cemetery. He often speaks about the residents in an aloof manner. Although his home and business are located in the very heart of the Northern Cemetery and is surrounded by decaying tombs, he has somehow convinced himself that since his home was built above a tomb that he should not be counted among the tomb dwellers of cemeteries. Even within this society there are many small distinctions that create a definitive form of social hierarchy.

Nasima Ali "Female Wisdom"

Nasima Ali was an elderly women who's size, charisma, and energy reflect her seventy plus years of austerity and poverty that she has witnessed in her lifetime. As a young teenager growing up in a poor area of Cairo, she was forced to become an adult at a very early age. As we sat down in the small dark one bedroom home, I was amazed at how easily and lucidly she was able to recall her life's events. In the eyes of many westerners her situation may seem dreary and miserable, however, with the typically deeply held religious perspective that many Egyptians hold, she doesn't view her life as a failure but one rather of blessings in which she can grow in wisdom and compassion.

Nasima states,"I attended school for only one year as it was customary in all of Egypt to keep the majority of women uneducated, however, even up to this day I don't have any regrets about my lack of education. Life has been my school, that is the most important education that one can receive and the best thing about it is that its free. As I travel to other parts of Cairo I observe how so many others have spent years and years attending some of the best schools and universities in Egypt, and yet know so little about the practicalities of day to day living what is really important is how one grows from experiences. People should learn to truly analyze and observe the world around them and in turn learn the deeper things about themselves. It really confuses me that people go and pay so much money to simply stick their faces in a book, they don't take care to really understand and relish the simple things that are often right under there noses. Being simplistic, patient, and pious is the true way in which they can acquire wisdom and take with them to the next life, the life after death!

Nasima's life was greatly transformed at the age of fifteen when she married and moved from a poor section of Giza, a small city famous for the pyramids, and moved to the cemetery with her husband. There she remains today, half a century later.

she told us that it may sound strange in your culture for someone to get married so young. In the cemeteries this is a very normal occurrence and I don't regret one day of it. I must be fair and mention that I didn't have much say in the decision of who I would marry. My father simply informed me one day that I was engaged, and that I would soon leave them and begin my new life with my husbands family. This was both exciting and frightening at the same time. During this time in Egypt marriage was the goal of almost every young girl my age, socially I was well prepared for it. Girls were socialized on how to be mothers and wives from a very young age. In our society and community the only thing that was truly important in those days were a women's ability to take care of the household duties and look after her families concerns. This is so different from today where girls are sent off into the work place and or to school to learn about things which really don't concern them and which distract from their true purposes.

Our decision to move to the cemetery was twofold: both idealistic and practical. Being newlyweds without any savings or strong income, the area provides a really cheap and convenient place to live. It was also practical in the sense that my husband was interested in finding work as a tomb keeper and undertaker. My first thoughts where what an ideal place to move! This may sound silly to a foreigner like you, however my primary concern about moving into the cemeteries where the jiin, or spirits of the dead that haunt this area. I was concerned about what would happen during the long hours in which my husband would be gone. Over time I have gotten use to living in close quarters to the jinn, they are my friends now, and with the help of Allah often act as my guides, warning me of upcoming dangers and sending me very strong omens through such things as dreams and vivid and timely thunder storms.

When we first moved here there were only a handful of people who had taken up permanent residence in this part of the cemetery. As you can now see, over the years many more people have come to live here and I am very pleased with our community. With the influx of new residence I know longer feel alone like I did in the old days. There are the trying times however when I think about my late husband and my children.

Nasima's husband died over fifteen years ago, yet she still continues to live in the same original room in which her and her husband shared all of there hopes, wishes, and dreams. I mentioned that in the west once a spouse dies, the other person often sells the home and moves in order to not have to deal with painful memories. Every morning she gets up to carry out her household duties as well as those of her late husband. She says that she has never slept an entire day of her life, every day it's the same routine: To wake up at 5am, wash, pray, and eat something small for breakfast. I first complete the chores around my small bedroom before going on to wash clothes and other more strenuous chores.

One of the things that keeps her going with such a rigorous and redundant routine is her deep faith in God and her warm relationship with the surrounding saints. After she finishes her chores she heads over to one of her favorite tombs, that of the female saint of Sidi Gohara. She was the servant of the much more popular and famous saint known as Sayyida Nafisa,. Before the blessed Nafisa died, she told her followers that anyone who would come to visit her and pay their respects after she passes away should always first visit the tomb of her servant Sidi Gohara. Her words have obviously been taken to heart, as there are a multitude of pilgrims who visit the cemetery to pay spiritual homage to both ladies.

Nasima states," This is my favorite place in the cemetery aside from my own home. Being a caretaker to one of the most holy tombs in the cemeteries is a tremendous source of inspiration as well as faith. As we entered the tomb, we move over to the left hand side in order to not come into direct contact with the body and offend the sensibilities of pious Muslims. I sit and watch as she diligently begins to sweep the floor of the chamber and then splashes water outside the tomb's door in order to prevent dust from permeating the air. When finished she comes and sits next to me under the shade and finally rests her aged body. She says that its here that she spends the majority of days, simply waiting to greet any visitor who come to pay respects to the dead. She eagerly awaits the company that will soon visit.

Nasima speaks with great passion and pride about her family to anyone that is patient enough to wait for her. She states, "I have one son and one daughter. I felt that my life was complete once I delivered a son to my husband. In the City of the Dead, children are the greatest source of joy offered to a family. Despite the great poverty and challenges that we face, its through our children that we are inspired to continue. Hussein my son has even completed secondary school and now drives a taxi in Alexandria. We are proud of him for being able to care for his family and earn a decent living outside of the cemeteries. We had to make many sacrifices in order for him to finish his education. Once he completed his schooling he started working as a clerk for a local government agency. He is now working in a field that has nothing to do with what he studied in school. Now you understand my disenchantment with education, I told you that education is not important in Egypt. Look what it got my son after so many years of hard work and sacrifices.

When his father died, Hussein fulfilled his duties as the only son by taking over his fathers responsibilities. During this time he realized that working as a tomb keeper and undertaker is actually more profitable than his government position. Our house would have been too small for him to stay once he was married and had a family of his own. His wife pressured him against my will to move to Alexandria and find what she considered decent work! Once moving to Alexandria he then wanted me to come live with him and his family, but I didn't want to leave this place which I called home for so many years. I didn't accept his request because I didn't want to be a burden on them, and I have my spiritual responsibilities to Allah and to the saint Sidi Gohara. My son comes a visits often and also sends money when he can.

Nasima says that, despite her solitary and simple lifestyle she is content with her life and feels a deep spiritual connection with the cemeteries, it would be her wish to die here.

She states, "Despite the object poverty and deep challenges that come with living here, I enjoy the fresh air and relatively peaceful atmosphere that you'd never experience in the heart of downtown Cairo. I also enjoy the familiarity of this community. Our challenges and difficulties have brought us closer together. I can honestly say that there is a genuine concern about ones fellow neighbor here. Those who live in the more affluent areas of Cairo waste too much time in always thinking about themselves and material issues, they have lost the meaning of family and what it means to appreciate the simply things in life, things that are closest to god. The atmosphere among us is not like that of a large city, rather it is much more like a small village where everyone knows each other and truly cares about one another.

After interviewing Nasima, I felt truly inspired and actually a little envious of the close sense of community and overall optimism in how she describes her life in the cemeteries. Having a background in journalism, I am well aware that there are usually two, three, or four sides to a story. There is always more than meets the eye, the more one scratches the surface here the richer and more complex the stories become.

My interpreter and I were once again on the prowl looking to interview a younger woman, perhaps one who may not have found such deep reference and stoic commitment in living in such a marginalized area of the world, perhaps a women that was not satisfied with being limited in what seems to be such a strong patriarchal society. As the evening wound down we went to a small nearby kiosk and had the good fortune of meeting Fatima Hassan.

Fatima Hassan was a tall, frail almost sickly looking women in her early twenties, but one whose discontent with life had caused her to look much older. She had flushed pale skin and heavy bags beneath her eyes. Her amber eyes had a look of restless discontent and deep seated resentment of someone that was at odds with the hand that life had gave them. Even with her little daughter wrapped tightly in her arms, Fatima seemed to be in perpetual motion like a caged cat in the zoo, ready to escape her surroundings at the first chance given. Her baby sat there facilitating between a quiet almost unresponsiveness to a whimpering discomfort. Once she began to speak about her life, she shed light on the somewhat strange and puzzling sides to her behavior.

Fatima states, "I was born in a small village in the Upper Egypt, close to the ancient town of Luxor about twenty four years ago. My childhood was spent working on a small farm with my ten siblings and my mother. My father had passed before I was three years old from natural causes. My only relationship with him came through photos and stories from my mother and grandmother. Hours would go by and I would have nothing to do except making sure that the cows were attended to. I have very fond memories of those days. The majority of my time was spent doing domestic work with my mother and grandmother. I was given all sorts of tasks, mostly things like fetching, carrying, and taking food to the men outside. In those days, life was simple and there was a tangible sense of security and predictability.

I was the youngest girl of the family, the second youngest of all of my siblings. As time passed my mother became ill so I was left with the responsibility of attending to her and all of the household duties. I actually enjoyed running the household since it was very good practice for me for my future when I would marry and have a husband and home of my own. It brings me great pain to think back to these days, when things were much simpler and everything was encased in innocence and youthful wonder. God, how I wish that I could go back in time and be a little girl again. Its was so easy then, whereas now I often feel overwhelmed by the challenges that face me in life.

I was married in the small village at the age of fifteen, I actually had little choice in the matter, it was already decided by my parents and extended family years before I could even put a sentence together. My father and his brother had actually agreed that there would be a marriage between their youngest children before I was born. This is very much part of the traditional way of marriage in the country side: people there believe that such an arrangement makes for a strong foundation and honorable marriage. The important thing is that a husband and wife know each other's background, character, and families because they are usually close relatives. Here in Cairo, however, this is not an easy thing to do. Its very difficult to arrange to marry relatives in the city or even here in the cemeteries because people don't have many family kin living close by, but ideally this is what the majority of people desire within my community. I come from a very close family and we are all tied to one another by many different marriages, mostly between cousins. Although the children of my generation were close in terms of blood and family, we were disengaged from one another as people.

When my husband came to meet me and my family before the wedding, I felt very uncomfortable. Although he was a blood relative he felt like a complete stranger. I had very vague memories of him from my childhood, and I could also sense that he felt that I was alien as well. Ironically our first meeting was a very awkward and embarrassing meeting between two strangers who would soon be life partners. The rest of the family seemed to be lost in the oblivion of the celebration and feast which would last over two days and nights. As usual we women prepared the feast. Even though I was the bride I still was not exempt from completing my family's obligation of cooking and cleaning. I felt lonely and fearful even amid my rejoicing family. I should have been happy as a bride to be, but I remember that evening having the worst ache in the bottom of my stomach, I was nervous and extremely unsettled.

The day before my actual wedding night, I had my haired oiled and henna applied to my hands and feet. Beside these superficial preparations, I was lectured by both my mother, who was bedridden, and my aunts about intimate things such as sex, marriage, and what things men expected from women. I must admit that this conversation made me very uncomfortable and insecure. They told me to appear scared but not hysterical as this could alarm my husband and actually offend him. Kamal did all the things I had been told to expect and seemed fairly satisfied with me afterwards. I wept and bled, giving him proof of my virginity. I remember thinking how ironic and paradoxical life had become: I was the wife of a man I hardly knew, yet everyone else pretended as if we were the oldest of companions!

The ceremony that Fatima is speaking about is often referred to as Doxla in Arabic. It is a tradition that is still practiced widely in both the City of Dead and Egypt in general. It involves the bridegroom breaking the woman's hymen with a forefinger wrapped in a piece of cotton loin. This usually transpires during the wedding feast in the presence of the bride's close female relatives. Guests at the feast usually wait outside the bedroom door until the triumphant bride's kin and the groom appear to actually present the blood –stained cloth for inspection. Then it is often ceremonially passed around before the festivities begin again. The couple may return to join the festival at this stage before the marriage is fully consummated. This is said to be because family members want proof that the bride actually bled and wept during this ceremony, as extra prove of the brides ignorance and innocence of sexual activity.

Fatima states, "In the beginning my husband's parents where very warm and welcoming to me. No one told me until after the wedding that my husband was taking me to live in the cemetery. It was a nightmare, I was leaving everything familiar and comfortable,. my sick mother, my siblings, the animals, and most importantly my dead father as well as all my family members that were buried on this land. I was an emotional mess, crying all of time, overwhelmed by feelings of guilt and remorse. For the first time my mother in law chastised me for not being able to hold back my tears. I remember this time of my life in which I felt terribly alone and abandoned. My husband also became very tough on me, criticizing everything that I did or didn't do.

I really didn't begin my marriage life on a good footing. The first meal that I prepared for my husband turned out to be a disaster. I over- cooked the meat and the entire house smelled of old smoke and burnt sauce. I was so embarrassed, not only for myself but also for my family, my mother had taught me not only how to cook, but also how to efficiently run a house- hold. This was surely the beginning of my battle with failure and a negative self conception. In the beginning I was still hopeful that our growing love would be enough to sustain us until our situation improved and we would be able to move out of this dreadful place.

Looking back in retrospect I can see that I had hoped for too much, even my vague wish that our intimacy we would grow as husband and wife would be a silly notion. Kamal and I started out as strangers despite our blood kinship, and we never progressed any closer. Perhaps deep down inside we both wanted to be closer, both emotionally and physically, but because of tradition we were ashamed because we didn't know how to make this happen. This is the price that one often pays in order to keep up appearances.

During the years of our marriage, Kamal didn't speak with me for weeks on end. He often behaved as if I were invisible. This really scared me as I had not been with a man before and automatically begin to fear that he was trying to get rid of me. This surely would have been easy, since I didn't know anyone and the cemetery was so huge and overwhelmingly foreign to me. For someone like myself coming from a very small village, crowded places can often be frightening. We were constantly surrounded by people here in Qarafa, yet and still I felt a deep sense of desolation and loneliness.

The great sense of neglect was soon to come to an end. About two months after living in the cemetery I met a wonderfully wise and mature lady named Amina Nasir. I was washing cloths one morning and in the midst of deep sobbing I was approached by an older, elegant women with streaking grayish white hair. She called out to me and asked me if I was okay? I remember trying to fight back my tears but failing to do so, she came over to me, grabbed me by the arm and asked me to sit down. She then invited me over to her small home which was actually right next door from ours. She introduced herself to me, helped me inside, and made me jasmine tea. It had been a long time since I had heard someone speak to me with such warmth and sincerity. It was as if I had been hypnotized by her kindness, which for a brief moment, reminded me of my mother. I was very nervous and unsure of myself. I was actually frightened to find out what would happen if my husband came home and saw that I hadn't finished the laundry, yet I was comfortable socializing with this strange women! Amina seemed to intuitively sense my discomfort and recommended that I relax. She said that she wanted to show me something outside. We walked for what seemed to be an eternity until arriving

at the local market place not very far from a large mosque. I was shocked in the way that women were acting in the market: you would never see such behavior in my small village. There was a great deal of noise and chaos, some of the women even shouted at the men who were selling things. There were so many strange and wonderful experiences in those early days.

After purchasing some fruit, she than announced that she wanted to meet with my husband. These words sent shock waves down my spine.

The fact that a women, even a wise, strong, and intelligent woman such as Amina, would ever be bold enough to initiate a meeting with a strange man was completely foreign to me.

Upon entering our home, I wasn't sure if my husband was happy or angry with me when I returned with a huge basket of food and a very open and talkative old woman. He, at least, pretended to be polite and friendly, and I in return, pretended to be happy to see him as if it were the first time. The two of them seemed to get along well and became engrossed in conversation while I made tea and prepared a light meal. I can remember the evening with great joy, and it was actually the first time that I was happy since living my parents village.

Kamal had decided to fix up the house in which we lived in, either in expectation that we were having children, or to keep up with the neighbors. Looking back in retrospect, I think that it was probably a mixture of both. He found a job in another district and went off to work there every day. There really was a lot of new synergy between us after I became pregnant. This allowed him or forced him to show a lot more affection and concern. During my pregnancy I became very ill, however because of my fear of disappointing my husband I pretended to be well. In retrospect this caused all kinds of added problems. Amina was a tremendous help during my pregnancy because she would help me with the cooking and the overall maintenance of my home while my husband was away.

Even though my husband pretends to be polite when I brought friends over, deep down inside he didn't like me making acquaintance and he is always criticizing the behavior of other women that live in the cemetery. What he didn't understand is that women here don't have the luxury or time to be overly concerned about tradition, modesty, or even certain morals when they're busy trying to simply survive and feed their families. His working many hours allowed me a certain sense of freedom, but I never disrespected or disobeyed him openly. During this period of my life I depended heavily on my female friends for emotional support and companionship.

Some life events can really test one's faith in God. We had a baby son named Omar that died three months after his birth. My entire world was shocked and I was numb for a very long time. Although I knew that we could have another baby, the memory of my first born son will always haunt me as if some dreadful reminder of god's disapproval of my marriage, or maybe as a subconscious hint of my own ineptitude at being a good wife and mother. Although I now have another child, a girl five months old named Shamia, a mother truly never recovers from the loss of a son.

My husband is a complete stranger who sometimes shares my bed but has nothing to do with any other part of my life. I have accepted this as my fate and now have a lovely daughter to look after and care for. I will never forget this tragedy and must try to cope the best way that I can. I honestly try to make the best of life and not give into self pity and self despair. Many people believe that it's a sin against god to dwell in self pity, for this life is transitory and every challenge, every pain felt is a test as well as a gift to god. If there were a way in which I could make life easier for my family and myself I would, but perhaps it's simply my destiny to achieve wisdom and strength in this life, Allah willing.

She then quietly fed her little girl while we finished up our tea. At this point there was a feeling from all of us that there was actually no more to be said, she had expressed all she could, all that could be shared was shared. We thank her and also left some money which was mandatory after interviewing and especially after visiting a home here in the City of Dead.

Soon after talking with Nasima we were greeted by her cousin named Abdul-Latif. He seemed to be in his in mid 30's, medium built, with a very anxious persona. He was very keen to know all about my interpreter and myself. After speaking with his cousin for a couple of minutes he quickly came back outside and told us that he had something very interesting to share. When ask what it was he became verbally vague, instead preferring to hurry us down another narrow cross section into an open yard. There he lifted a flat board which was on the edge of an old wooden shack. When he lifted the board he took out what look like dirty bottles with old brown worn paper inside. Abdul-Latif describe these lettered bottles as notes to the dead! Among the more bizarre surviving cultural practices in Cairo's cemetery communities are the hand written letters sent to the deceased. As in ancient times,

Egyptians write to a deceased close relative often sharing their troubles and asking for guidance and intervention. The majority of these appeals are made to a holy saint, prophet, or more commonly a venerated dead person within the community. The person is thus claiming from God the ovation of the venerated dead to have a prayer answered.

The modern day obituary pages of Egyptian newspapers are filled with letters to the dead like a grateful farewell, expressing both joy and sorrow, wishing them peace in the eternal after life. Another popular way of communicating with the departed is called istikhara or (inducing dreams). On the days when they visit these holy tombs, residents will normally place his or her right hand over the top of the tombstone and give a prayer.

The funerary foundation named Waqf:

Of the many examples reflecting the presence of ancient Egypt on the culture of the cemeteries is a practice called Waqf in Arabic or endowment system in English. The roots of this practice can be traced directly back to the mortuary cults that flourished in the days of the pharaohs.

The very structure and dynamics of a death cult meant having to regularly keep stocks of food for the deceased, who were thought of by the community as continuing to have the same needs in the after life as they had in this world. According to Christel Kessler, even during ancient times the deceased were already taking precious material gifts with them into the tomb. Their direct heirs, usually the first born sons, were responsible for ensuring the upkeep of the grave. In Cairo's city of the Dead, this duty usually proved to be financially beyond the means of the living. With each generation, cults of the dead proliferated. This eventually led to the creation of the funerary foundation, which consisted of allocating to a dead person's mortuary cult a property whose proceeds were to be directed back into that cult.

Originally this privilege was reserved only for members belonging to the royal family, nobles, and land owners. The system was later extended to the entire common population. In turn every Egyptian had his/her own means with which to ensure the sustainability of a future mortuary cult before she died. Any that could afford it set up a small foundation with a resident priest to perform the necessary rituals and make sure there were enough offerings around the tomb.

These funerary foundations were dropped at the end of the Pharaonic era, after which the only duties of the living toward their dead were to perform a libation of symbolic water sacrifice every nine days. Also very important is the chanting of the name of the deceased. This is said to be done in order to give them, in the final moment of their great transition, another few moments of glorious redemption.

It wasn't until after the tenth century that the Fatimids revived the system to ensure the upkeep and integrity of the magnificent tombs, mausoleas, and mosques built in the city of the dead. Funerary foundations also, by extension, came to ensure a livelihood for the donor's designated heirs and the staff charged with the maintenance of those elaborate tombs. There had to be enough to cover the vast offerings for the poor and the needy on special days and pay the spiritual Qur'anic chanters to lead prayers and rituals, many times at the exclusion of the poor.

Islamic tradition believes the dead in their graves profit from every prayer that is chanted for them. Many Muslim residence of the cemeteries seek to avoid a second death in the grave by appealing for food, gifts, and other material values in order to escape their perceived punishment in the afterlife. Since the Ancient Pharaonic days, the wording may have changed, but the believe remains almost exactly the same.

Impotence in the face of the greatest mystery (death), the inequalities and injustices reigning over the earth, and the sadness and sense of deep separation from our known realities, have driven human societies to develop rites and rituals that have remained unchanged to this day. Both Islamic and Coptic funerary custom is no more than a variant of ancient pagan practices. Not all of the cultural practices in the City of the Dead hark back to ancient Egypt, however reactions to the universal phenomenon of death have been broadly similar, notwithstanding distinctive cultural, regional, and ethnic customs.

In comparison, more modern acreage of Egypt and certainly the West, have entailed a certain indifference if not fear, towards death and any religious ritual relating to the afterlife. In Cairo's Cemeteries, the Tombs and funerary architecture still shape part of the urban landscape and continue to enjoy a significant amount of care and attention from the living. Here, possibly more than any other place on earth, with its disproportionate scale of cemeteries, funerary complexes, huge and diverse tombs designed as idealized replicas of homes for the living, one can truly observe the multifunction nature of a city designed for both the living and dead.

After conducting these personal interviews, I felt as if I truly had a greater insight and better understanding of the challenges of the everyday people that live in this community. More than any of the great monuments, tombs, or even cultural events, visiting the homes of the average person living here truly created a vision of reality and a cultural empathy which helped to transform and overcome any sense of isolation or strangeness that I may have felt in the beginning.

Chapter 6
The Citadel, "The ancient fortress that still haunts Cairo"

"Nothing is born which death makes not subject of his state."
—Bhartrhari

Of all the great monuments that tower of the City over the Dead, one truly holds the keys to understanding its complexity, mystery, history and people, this monument is known today as the Citadel of Cairo. Construction on the Citadel actually began in 1176 under the supervision of the famous Salah Ad-Din who was made famous in the West by the myriad of Crusades in which he fought against. Legend has it that Salah Ad-Din chose the site for its healthy air. The story goes that he hung meat up all around Cairo. Everywhere the meat spoilt within a day, with the exception of the Citadel area where it remained fresh for a week. In Reality this location was chosen because it provided a strategic advantage both to dominate Cairo as well as to defend it from foreign invasion

In fact, the Citadel was constructed by using the most up- to- date castle building technology that had developed out of nearly 100 years of warfare against the Crusaders. Its dressed stone walls are ten meters high and three meters thick. Where ever possible, they were built on rock, above ground level, to prevent undermining, which was actually the most effective means of breaching fortifications during a medieval siege. Small half- round towers with thick inner chambers, project from the outer façade every 100 meters, allowing the defending garrison to direct flanking fire against enemy soldiers trying to scale the walls. The towers are connected by upper ramparts, once protected by crenellation and interior corridors, which ran the full length of the Citadel's original 2,000-meter circumference. The corridors contain small rooms, every ten meters, with windows that allow archers to shoot at enemies from the safety of the inner walls.

The northeastern corner o the Citadel juts out from the rest of the enclosure, dominating the pass cut between the fortress and Muqattam hills. An invading army could only by pass the walls of Cairo by entering this narrow corridor, which is controlled by two towers, the Sand Tower and the Blacksmith's Tower.

The Citadel originally had three major entrances. The Gate of the Steps, on its northwestern side, was the main public entrance, giving access from the city. It was approached by a sloping ramp road, leading to both fortified gates separated by a curving flight of steep stairs cut into the rock of the Citadel hill. Only the domed vestibule of the upper gate survives. The other gates are on the east and south sides of the enclosure. Both protected by twin towers and bent entrance ways for maximum defense. The most mysterious entrance way is named "Bab Al-Qarafa or Cemetery Gate, named after the burial grounds in the vicinity of the fortress.

The eastern gate is today known by its eighteenth century name, the Gate of the Imam. It faces the Muqattam hills and is the entrance most exposed to enemy attacks. In order to protect it against battery rams, it was built above ground level and is reached by way of a bridge across a sixteen-meter wide moat.

If foreign enemies managed to penetrate either of these gates, they would find themselves within an open court, surrounded by inner walls lined with archers. Those who did survive this death- trap still had to manage a ninety degree turn into a tunnel, protected by a second gate, before they could reach the interior of the Citadel. A small number of postern gates are also located around the fortress, enabling the defending garrison to make surprise sorties against the enemy's position outside the walls. Within the complex there is the huge Bir Yusuf Salah well. Built some 285 feet deep through solid rock in order to supply the occupants of the fortress with an inexhaustible supply of drinking water. This well is not simply a shaft, like everything else in the Citadel, there is always more than meets the eye. Here is a ramp large enough for animals to descend into the well in order to power the machinery that lifted the water. Unfortunately the well is closed to tourist these days.

Salah Ad Din, was a very unique leader for his time. He was born in 1138 and was actually a Kurd who became famous world wide for his mission of reuniting Egypt, Iraq, and Syria and nearly succeeding in driving the incursive European Crusaders out of the Holy Land.. One can argue that his overall visions elevated him above the petty ambitions of the day. He was often ruthless and shrewd in his dealings with others, but many believe that he made a sincere effort to base his life off the spiritual principles of Islam. Ruling in an age when perfidy was the norm, he never broke a promise or truce with either his Muslim friends or Christian enemies. Although of simple, even austere needs himself, he was generous to a fault with his followers. He was accessible to everyone, even in moments of great exhaustion. He devoted the same care to listening to complaints of his troops as to assisting a Christian mother in finding her captive child. When the crusaders took Jerusalem in 1099, the rumor is that they murdered virtually all of its inhabitants, boasting that parts of the city were knee-high in blood. After he re-took the city in 1187, he spared his victims, giving them time to leave and a safe passage, it was after all, a holy city and this should be fought as a just war in his eyes.

In the end it was the strength of Salah Ad-Din's character, rather than the size of his army, that really shaped and sealed the history of the Citadel. By 1186 he had conquered and defeated his fellow Muslim rivals and could now focus on his most cherished dream: The elimination of the Christian crusaders throughout the Middles East. Ironically this sounds eerily familiar today with many of the Islamic fundamentalist who claim a similar goal towards the modern West. The following year he and his army invaded the Latin kingdom with 20,000 soldiers and trapped the entire Crusader army next to the sea of Galilee. During the ensuing battle of Hattin, the Christians were decisively defeated, with their king and their most sacred relic a fragment of the True Cross, falling to Salah Ad-Din. This Islamic victory, was followed by the capture of Jerusalem and conquest of the entire Latin Kingdom within the Middle East.

News of the great defeat sent shock waves throughout Europe. The most powerful leaders of Europe, Richard the Lionhearted of England, Frederick Barbarossa of Germany, and Philip August of France, all gathered their armies and set sail for Palestine in order to win back the Holy Land for Christendom. This third crusade would prove to be the most challenging that he would have to face. His army was built around a number of semi-independent military contingents led by his principle commanders, many of the them having deep roots here in Qarafa. Each commander maintained his own army from revenues he received from a feudal land grant here in the cemeteries.

Salah Ad-Din, confronted by the invasion of a determined, well-organized and financed enemy, was forced to keep his army in the field continuously for three years. The prolonged conflict was a serious test on the financial, emotional, and structural resources of the empire, which throughout these hostilities, was in danger of collapsing under the relentless assault of the crusaders. A true testament to both his courage and leadership skills, he was able to hold his feudal levies together and finally fight his Christian opponents to a standstill.

After the last of the Crusading rulers left for home in 1192, the Christians controlled only a narrow strip of the Palestinian coast. Although the Latin Kingdom would survive for another 100 years, its power had been broken forever. His life work completed, Salah Ad-Din died the following year in Damascus. His generosity, courage, and honestly made him a legendary figure in his own lifetime, admired as much by his Christian foes as by his Muslim admirers. Even the great European poet, Dante placed him, not in the pit of hell with other infidel villains, but in the same company of Hector and Aeneas in the limbo reserved for virtuous pagans. Yes this great figure who is such a folk hero within the City of Dead, extended his greatness not only to the borders of Cairo, but out into the world!

After his death Salah Ad Din's nephew, Al-Kamil, reinforced the Citadel by enlarging several of the towers. He went on the build the huge Burg al-Haddad (Blacksmith's Tower) and the Burgar-Ramlab (Sand Tower) making them three times larger. These two structures controlled the narrow pass between the Citadel and the cemeteries. Al-Kamil also built a number of towers around the perimeter of the walls, three of which can still be seen overlooking the citadel parking area right between the opening gates. These massive structures were square, up to twenty five meters (eighty feet) tall and thirty meters (one hundred feet) wide. In 1218, upon the death of his father, the son now moved his residence to the palace in what is now the Southern Enclosure.

After the Mamluks finally overthrew the Ayyubid rulers in 1250, their sultan (king) Baybars al Bunduqdari (1260-77) moved into the palace. He isolated the area by building a huge wall that divided the fortress into two separate enclosures linked by the gate al Qullah. The area where the palace once stood is called the Southern Enclosure, while the larger part of the Citadel proper is referred to as the Northern Enclosure.

Al- Nasir Muhammad the Sultan who tore down most of the earlier buildings in the Southern Enclosure and replaced them with considerably gander structures. Today the only remaining structure built by him is the Al-Nasir Mohammed Mosque. This mosque was the royal mosque for both the Citadel and cemeteries, as it was here that the ancient rulers of Cairo performed their Friday prayers. It was large enough to hold up too five
thousand worshippers.

From its very inception the mosque was built on a site considered to be very holy ground. The earlier shrine may have been an Arab congregation, perhaps even built by Salah himself. Although there were several sacred buildings built within the walls of the Citadel, that of Sultan al-Nasir was one of the most glamorous in Cairo until the original dome collapsed in the sixteenth century.

This hypostyle mosque is built as a regular free- standing rectangle around a courtyard with a large dome covering the prayer niche area. Three entrances including one on the northeastern side with a rounded shallow recess and another on the northwestern wall with a stalactite portal. The third entrance on the Southern wall is adorned with a pointed arch, including a sun-rise motif in ablaq masonry. None of the entrances has benches, making them the exception of the rule in Cairo.

Unlike other mosques within this city, the facades of this one are not paneled and has no decoration except its crenellation. Its appearance is rather austere except for the two exotic minarets at the northeast corner. The position of the two minarets and two asymmetrically located portals are dictated by the orientation and design of the mosque. They each face the northern enclosure of the Citadel on one side and adjoins the residences of the sultan on the west and south. The minaret to the north directed its call of prayer to the officers and soldiers dwelling there. The other tower faced the sultan's palace. The northern minaret is the taller of the two. Both of these wonderfully constructed structures are built entirely of stone.

The western tower is conical, with a shaft carved in a deep zigzag motif that is vertical on the first story and horizontal on the second, its top is completely unique for all of Egypt. It has no openings and has a garlic-shaped bulb resting on a ribbed, tapered cylinder. The entire upper structure is covered with beautifully structured and designed mosaics like those found at al-Nasir's mosque. A beautiful Quranic inscription band made of white mosaic adorns the nick of the bulb. This minaret actually continues the ancient tradition of placing minarets at the portals of foundations. Its location at the western portal, which was the ceremonial entrance facing the sultan's apartments, accounts for the distinguishing of its shafts from those of northeastern minaret with a completely different shape. The base is rectangular and second story is cylindrical. Both are without carving. Its upper part has an open hexagonal pavilion that supports the top of the structure, which is similar to the top of the western minaret. Each tower has a balcony that is pierced with Islamic symbols and carved in the same technique used to make other parts of the castle. The crenellation around the bulbous top of this minaret is the earliest known experimentation with this technique.

A folklore states that a craftsman from Tabriz, Persia, came to Cairo during the reign of Al-Nasir and built the minarets with faience, as was the fashion in Persia. Each of these structures also have another common feature that distinguish them from all others, their foundations are below the level of the roof indicating that the minarets were already standing.

Deep into the mosque the walls are supported by the arcades of arched windows that give the building its special character. These portals were obviously added when the roof was raised. The openings help reduce the thrust carried by the arches, admit light, and play an ornamental role as well. The designs of the arcades are composed of similar masonry as the stones. Down the outdoor courtyard and through the rounded door ways one walks under beautifully decorated mabkharas, (incense burners). They are both mysterious and beautiful, encapsulating the special collection of pre-Islamic crowns of the mosque. The two pairs of Coptic Christian capitals at the main entrance are particularly interesting. The white marble carved with a basket pattern joins other designs dating to the Roman and Greek periods.

In the beginning, this complex had a number of large iron-grilled windows that are now walled up. It was also designed with intricately sculpted marble dados which were later removed by Sultan Seleem (The Grim) and shipped to Istanbul with other marbles from the palace. Today the ground level within the Citadel has risen, so the mosque must have originally been at a much higher level and reached by a staircase. To the north is a huge dome that rises above a prayer niche. The original dome was made of solid copper and is carried by granite columns like those of the Citadel palaces. These original pillars were taken from ancient Egyptian temples. As the transition zone is made of wood, it would be safe to assume that the original dome, like many others found in The City of the Dead, was made of plastered wood.

The Al-Nasir Muhammad mosque has another interesting feature which consist of a small loggia located above the northwestern entrance. It is perhaps a large circular bend, like the bench on columns in the sanctuary of other mosques that is used for calls to prayer, recitations and Quran readings.

Much of the architecture that can be found in the Citadel was built during the Ottoman (ancient Turkish) occupation. The ottomans actually rebuilt the wall that separates the Northern and Southern Enclosures, as well as the Bab al-Quallah. They also constructed the largest tower in the today's Citadel, The Burg al-Muqattam, which rises above the entrance to the Citadel of Salah Saalem Highway. It measures 80ft and has a diameter of 24 meters or 79ft.

From the late sixteenth century until the French occupation, the strict military structure of the Ottoman soldiers gradually deteriorated. During this period, the Azab troops began to marry, and were even allowed to build their own housing within the fortress. By the mid seventeenth century, the Citadel had become an enclosed residential district with private shops, huge commercial enterprises, as well as public baths.

Another famous or rather infamous leader that resided within the Citadel, was Ottoman ruler Muhammad Ali Pasha. One of the great builders of Modern Egypt, who came to power in 1805. He was responsible for considerable alteration and re- building within the Citadel. He redesigned much of the outer walls and replaced many of the decaying interior buildings. He also reversed the roles of the Northern and Southern Enclosures, making the Northern Enclosure his private domain, while the Southern Enclosure became opened to the public. The famous Mohammed Ali Mosque, which was constructed in the style of Ottoman Baroque, reflects the great religious shrines of Turkey.

Within the Citadel is a National Police Museum. Constructed over the site of the Palace just opposite the Mosque. Its vivid and memorable displays of law enforcement date back to the dynastic period. Upon entering the museum I was greeted by a tall muscular security guard that introduced himself as Mohammed. He ask me if I was from England, I smiled and laugh and stated that I was actually from the United States. He said that he has a sister in law studying in Houston Texas and that he one day hopes to visit. In typical Egyptian fashion Mr. Mohammed offered me a cup of tea and motioned me to sit with him. After walking around the Citadel all afternoon I was actually in the mood to take a rest and just kick back.

The view from this museum was actually spectacular and on this clear day it seemed as if I could see all over the entire cemeteries. Mr. Mohammed said that he grew up in a section of the city called Maadi. I laughed and let him know that I also lived in there. Its a very upscale section of Cairo that is an enclave for American and other expiates that work and live in Cairo. I got the strong sense that he was raised in an upper middle class Egyptian family, not only because of his place of residence, but also by his gentile and articulate tone. He then asked me if I was simply taking a tour of the Citadel or doing more extensive research. I told him that I was actually writing a book on its history, rulers, and most importantly its relationship with the City of Dead

He sullenly shook his head and stated that the two places were inseparable and deeply intertwined. He said that although the Citadel belong to all of Cairo, her roots and foundation will always be connected to cemeteries. Mr. Mohammed stated that the citadel was the bridge in which the very soul of this community expressed itself to the world. I finished my tea and took a long deep look outside over the Qarafa and felt the strange sensation as if I had been transported back in time. I looked at my watch and realized that I needed to continue my research tour.

walking through the Northern Gate I came across the Muhammad Ali Harem Palace. Built in the same Ottoman style as the Jewel Palace, its initial use was as a residence for this sultan's many wives. This area also served as a military hospital during the British occupation and was only returned to Egyptian control after World War Two. Since 1949, it has been used as the Military Museum of Egypt. A myriad of diverse displays cover the military history of Egypt during all different periods of the country's history, one of the most interesting displays is the Summer Room which contains an elaborate system of marble fountains, basins, and channels meant as a cooling systems. It is probably the last such example in Cairo. Behind the carriage gate of the museum is one of the largest of the square towers built in 1207.

Near the far end of the Northern enclosure is the Suleyman Pasha Mosque. It was the first Ottoman style mosque built in Egypt and dates from 1528. it was built to serve the early Ottoman (Turkish) troops. Today the Citadel is one of the main attractions, not just in the city of dead but in all of Cairo. Within its huge walls are to be found the very stories that make Cairo so near and tangible. However behind the noble deeds and heroic leaders that once occupied this castle, there lies a hidden, darker, more nefarious history. One that is sometimes deliberately overlooked or concealed.

Getting back to the military history of this time, we have to look that the finished legacy of Salah Ad Din's son. With the memory of the Third Crusade still fresh in his mind, Al-Kamil abandoned the aggressive foreign policy of his father, and devoted himself to consolidating the defenses of his empire.

He constructed a number of massive square keeps, up to 25 meters high and 30 meters wide, around the perimeter of the Citadel. Two overlooked the Gate of the steps and three more were built straddling the Citadel's southern wall, where a rise in the ground level makes this section of the fortress particularly vulnerable to battering rams and undermining. The square towers are filled with interior halls and corridors, which acted as command posts, storage areas and barracks. They formed a ring of self contained forts around the walls of the Citadel, designed to function independently during a siege.

Before Al-Kamil's new palace was completed, he was confronted by the invasion of the Fourth Crusade. He was able to defeat the Christians in 1221, but only after a grueling three year struggle. To avoid a repetition of the experience, he came to an accord in 1229 with Emperor Frederick the second, the leader of the German Crusaders. Jerusalem was declared an open city, accessible to Muslims and Christians alike. This enlightened compromise proved unpopular with religious fanatics on both sides and hostilities were soon resumed.

Upon his death however in 1238, the surviving princes began fighting among themselves for control of the empire. By 1240, Al Kamil's eldest son, Al-Salih, had established himself as new sultan of Egypt, but his ruthless rise to power had isolated him from the support of the masses.

Realizing he could no longer depend on political support of his community, Al- Salih began to raise an army large enough to defend his country against another Crusade from the West, as well as from the looming threat of the Mongol hordes of Genghiz Khan. Ironically the bulk of his soldiers were freemen commanded by Kurdish kings from modern day Iraq. The fighting abilities of these slave soldiers was put to the test in 1249, during the Sixth Crusade of St. Louis 1X of France. Egypt was invaded and the coastal city of Damietta was captured. AL Salih, then dying of tuberculosis, was carried in a coffin at the head of his army to the Delta town of Mansura in order to prevent a Crusade thrust on Cairo. He died just as the Christian Crusaders began their advance on Mansura. His death was concealed, however by his wife in order to maintain the morale of the Egyptian army.

Today the Citdadel sits as one of the ancient endowments of Cairo, who's haunting voice reflects a myriad of untold stories.

Niriman Ali and family

Wealthy styled tomb

Poverty styled tomb

Sealed Burial Chamber

Wall of Sultan Qaytbay's Madrassa

Niriman Ali's home near Tomb in Qarafa

Overview of Qarafa and Moqattam Hills

Tomb of Dhul-Nun al Misri" Southern Cemetery

Mosque and Madrassa of Sultan Hasan

Sufi Drummer

Whirling Dervish

Sufi Dancers

Snake vendor in Friday's Market

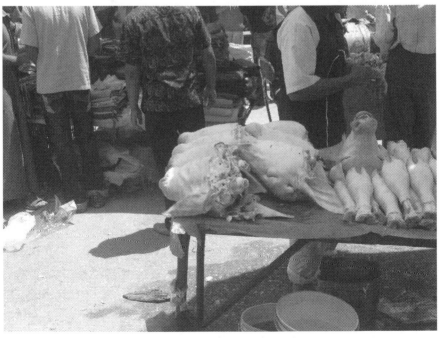

Scene from Friday's Market

Used Clothes auction in Friday's Market

Mosaic near the tomb of Shagar al Durr

Small entrance into City of the Dead

Nasima Ali and Niece

Residential burial Chamber

Outer wall burial Chamber

School boys from Qarafa

Tomb guardian Northern Cemetery

The Citadel viewed from Al Azhair Park

Chapter 7
Feeding the Dead

"He that begins to live, begins to die."
—Francis Quarles

I have mentioned in previous chapters that the original inhabitants of the City of Dead worked as tomb keepers for wealthy Egyptian families. During the early twentieth century the majority of the men in the cemeteries labored in the lime quarters that were eventually closed down. These trades continued to provide employment for the men within the city. With a dramatic increase in the population from rural villages of Egypt, these trades could no longer accommodate the increasing influx of people seeking work here. As the employment sector became more diverse, specialization in the labor force had virtually disappeared. Today the community is involved in a variety of diverse economic activities. A large number of the people have secured low paying jobs in the formal sector of Cairo's work force. Some residents have set up small informal businesses such as food stands and kiosk, (small movable shops), and even tea shops. The vast majority of the residents of the City of Dead are among the swelling ranks of Cairo's unemployed. Migration has transformed rural unemployment into urban unemployment. Many of the residents of the cemeteries do not hold one specific type of job for any length of time. The majority of able body men float from temporary job to temporary job, brining in money to their families by an means necessary. One very interesting fact is that the majority of people in Qarafa find creative and alternative means of employment in the informal economy. They sell used cloths, vegetables, wipe the dirt off of car windshields, shine shoes, and even sell exotic animals.

Similar to informal housing, the informal economy consist of those economic activities that are not officially noticed or recognized by the states government agencies. They are distinguished from the formal economic and social activities that are licensed and grow within the socialized institutions of the state. Informal economic activities range from individual actions such as hawking on street corners to small scale enterprises. The vast majority of the informal economic sectors are made up from people from marginalized groups of the society. As common sense would dictate: informal economic activities and informal housing often go hand and hand. Irregular economic activities are normally caused by the unreliability of employment as well as extremely low social mobility. Indeed this informal system is surely responsible for what many folks call the Egyptian Miracle, "a celebration of the day to day survival of this community".

There is a huge amount of activity taking place within these borders. Wandering around many of the back streets of this city, I observe traveling salesman transversing the streets and alleys yelling out the names of their wares, as young boys selling bottled gas run along calling out: to let everyone know they are coming. These so called informal salesman allow the women of the City of Dead to purchase many of their daily needs without traveling very far from their homes. There are even make-shift factories in the cemeteries, often noticeable by the streams of dark grey smoke rising among the tombs.

Walking in the Southern Cemetery during dusk, I observed young men making aluminum cups. They are covered from head to toe in black soot and yet perform their duties with joy and passion. They would laugh, joke, smile, and even take time out to tease me. One tall aqualine nosed man with piercing hazel eyes, called out to me in his broken English: Nubi, Nubi! This was surely a reference to my dark skin which is shared by many Nubians of upper Egypt. Most lighter skinned Arabs throughout Egypt have a tendency to categorize all black-skinned persons as being Nubian.

As I walked up the street I saw older men dressed in the traditional Islamic fittings repairing and painting cars among the tombs. I observed the fast moving and intimidating highway filled with young children running pass speeding cars simply trying fill the tires of the passing trucks in order to make extra money.

Between the large mosque and stone tombs there's a section that is so beautifully constructed that its hard to believe that this area is inside a cemetery. Not only is the street home to multitudes of tomb-dwelling residence, but interspersed among them are a small internet cafés, four barbershops, coffee shops, as well as a jewelry store. wandering thru the various neighborhoods I still ponder about the vast amounts of history that looks me in the face and seems to whisper a silent song of eternity.

As in many parts of rural and even urban Egypt, the City of the Dead is a deep reminder that the government of Egypt has chosen to largely ignore the situation of the masses of people living in poverty, perhaps wishing that the problems would simply disappear as in the old days when stories of the magic Jinns (dead spirits) would grant such wishes. Since it has been unable to provide a viable alternative solution to these illegal informal housing communities, the government has been forced to extend some services into the cemeteries over the years. For example, there are now public water taps in some areas, along with mini supermarkets, community telephones, and even some small internet services. Where public taps are nonexistent, residents here must buy water from vendors or they simply receive water from the nearby mosques.

For most residence gaining access to adequate and clean water supply is challenging at best. As I travel from one part the cemetery to another, I often observe groups of young women spending considerable amounts of time trying to retrieve clean water, which is so crucial to their cooking, cleaning and bathing needs.

Another really dreadful challenge that most face is living within the confines of a informal sewage system. Residents who have any sewage facilities usually have make-shift latrines with holding tanks for the disposal of toilet waste. Most residence cannot afford to have the tanks emptied by tanker vehicles, so they have little alternative other then having there own local sewage person collect for a small fee. This allows for the cemeteries to remain remarkably clean and also helps to create another source of employment.

All is not bleak however, because of the remarkable resiliency and determination of many of its residence, more and more folks have gained access to electricity and telephones. Public buses now traverse many of the Qarafa's' larger streets, or at least come into close proximity to them. Many of the roads that are now officially recognized by the government are kept paved. This community has become more secure with increased police presence and a very well defined social network that actually makes it one of the safest places in Cairo.

With no formal system of garbage removal I was very curious to know how the streets here were kept fairly clean. My interpreter and I were informed that there were a group of informal garbage collectors (known as the Zabaleen in Arabic), that help to keep the area clean and fill the gap that the government's official disposal system doesn't fill.

We ran into an older gentleman who ran a small jewelry shop here. He offered to explain the deeper reasons that garbage wasn't picked up officially by the Cairo government. He introduced himself as Ahmed and stated that he was known as the most honest man in the City of the Dead. I again repeated the question as to why the city of Cairo didn't bother to have an official sanitation system running thru the Cemeteries? He simply smiled and said that they tend to avoid the poorer areas of the city where garbage is less valuable for recycling, which in turn helps to sustain the wages of the low paid garbage collectors.

Another issue that I was curious to learn more about was health care. Speaking with the members of the community, It was very obvious that there faith was put more in the will of Allah (god) or even in local non- traditional healers as oppose of to traditional doctors. The majority of the people here live in dreadful fear of falling ill simply because of the lack of access to affordable health care. Most will avoid going to an official doctor until their health situation has progressed into a dire circumstance. Other residents who have grave sicknesses typically have to travel far outside the walls of the cemetery in order to receive any kind of official health attention. Mr. Ahmed stated that official government subsidized health care is available, however the vast majority of the people here don't trust it and tend to prefer the more unofficial healers that are so common throughout the cemeteries. Most people in this community have the perception that any doctor that chooses to work in Qarafa must be poorly trained and not very good at his/her profession. This attitude is an overall reflection of the deep overriding mistrust of the government. He also points out that for the average person living here, even subsidized health care is too expensive. He describes charlatans who actually make a living taking advantage of desperate and less informed people. These false physicians, as he calls them, often visit the cemeteries and present residents with counterfeit credentials and sometimes walk off with a persons small life savings, giving them quack and sometimes even dangerous medical advice.

Ahmed mentions that the majority of people fear falling ill and often pray that they can provide for their families if something were to happen. Most people here are supporting elderly parents who often need frequent and expensive medical attention. Ironically both of his elderly parents have chronic sicknesses that drain Ahmed's already meager income. His father suffers from acute respiratory disorder, yet and still he refuses to consult an official physician on a regular basis for fear of being taken advantage of.

Like the health care system, education remains a major challenge for the residents of the City of the Dead. Many of the people find the cost of education to be far too expensive and time consuming. I was shocked to find out that although there are a couple of Islamic institutes in the cemeteries, there is only one formal school in the entire cemeteries. Ahmed and others mention that although officially education is considered free within Egypt, the children of the Cemeteries face the challenge of most of Cairo's urban poor: schools that are overcrowded and under funded. Many schools have even begun to have two shifts during the day in order to reduce class size. Even with the double shifts he says that the majority of teaching turns simply into baby sitting, with student teacher ratio exceeding that 80-to-1. As a result only those who can afford private lessons receive a decent education.

Most residence say its very difficult for students to both work and study. There is usually inadequate levels of books, desk, and other necessary supplies for education. Because of these challenges within the official educational system, the vast majority of the citizens of the here have come to distrust it. Most parents observe that with the present challenges and lack of jobs, secondary or high school graduates fare little better than drops outs in Egypt's job market. As a result the majority of children in the cemeteries receive no more than a primary school education. Many families aspire instead to have there children find an apprenticeship or anything considered practical that will increase job skills and earning potential in the short term. You can walk through the community on any given week day and observe the majority of school age children helping there families out by running errands, often for a small kiosk that line most of the streets here.

My first view of this was repulsion and condemnation of the society which would deny its most vital resource the opportunity to get an education. One thing that travel teaches is the ability to be able to look at the culture from local eyes and not judge or impose one's own social norms and values upon it. I must admit that my research in the City of the Dead surely pushed this concept to the limit.

We turned down a very narrow dirt road in the heart of the Southern Cemetery where I observed a young man, no more than fifteen years old, working as a Barber. We asked him if he attends school? He lit up with a huge smile and said that he had to drop out two years ago in order to help support his family. He told us that he and his friends desired to learn English above anything else.

Male children are often chosen to learn a trade at a young age. Women also often neglected the right to get an education, but for different reasons. Girls are often taken out of school in order to learn how to run the household. If however education is seen as a way of increasing the daughters chances of getting married, then a family may consider leaving her in school. The average family considers it pertinent that a girl stay at home and learn how to run a household and successfully fulfill the traditional responsibilities of an Egyptian wife and mother. Looking at education as a way of increasing social mobility for women is a very new and almost revolutionary concept here in Qarafa, were traditional views are still very deeply imbedded.

We met a nineteen year old lady named Sheera who had a youthful face and happy, jovial, innocent eyes that seemed to light up whenever she spoke. She said that she was a single girl that had two years of secondary school, which is very rare for a female to accomplish here. She dropped out of school to actually help her family run a small tea shop. She feels that school is actually a waste of time and often precludes many young women from the opportunity of getting married. She believes that many of the subjects taught in school like business and politics, women have no right in learning about anyway. There are people in the cemeteries with educational degrees, however they are very much the exception rather than the rule. There are a myriad of challenges and obstacles that even transcend the economic hardships of living in the City of Dead. It's amazing to observe the day to day dynamics of how this community carries out its duties with warmth, dignity, and a deep reverence for family relationships, sometimes to their own detriment.

Chapter 8
The Madrasa of Hassan
and The Black Death

**"A Stone I died and rose again a plant, a plant I died and
rose an animal, I died an animal and was born a man.
Why should I fear ? What have I lost by death?"**
—Rumi

Within the City of the Dead, one the monuments that has
intrigued historians the most is the Mosque and Madrasa of
Sultan Hassan. This Mosque, which is located on the outskirts of the
Northern Cemetery, still towers above all the other mosques of Cairo.
There are many interesting stories about it, which many consider to be
one of the finest examples of early Islamic architecture. In fact many
writers consider this to be one of the premier examples of Islamic
monuments not only in Egypt, but in the entire Islamic world. The
founder of this gigantic monument was Sultan Hassan, the son of the
great mamluk ruler, Al Nasser.

Sultan Al Nasser had ruled continuously since the beginning of the
century, this set a record that has never been surpassed by any Egyptian
leader since. Despite his ruthlessness, (he had some 175 of his Amirs
killed and thousands of his other opponents tortured by cruelest means,)
Al Nasir's rule had been an interlude of stability and prosperity. During
his rule: the measurement of size, peace, and wealth, found in Cairo
was unrivalled anywhere in the known world. The ottoman Turks to
the north were not were not yet a threat, the Mongol menace from
the east had been subdued, and the Christian leaders of the west now

sent traders as oppose to warriors to the Egyptian capital. Even within his personal life things were as sweet as they've ever been. His twelve daughters each received a dowry of some 900,000 gold and silver dinars. His fourteen sons were considered to be the wealthiest in the world. Trouble however was lurking close by, during the seven short years that followed Al-Nasir's rule, disease, murder and intrigue eliminated five of his sons from the succession. Soon after his youngest son Hassan, a red haired, freckled face boy of thirteen, acceded to the throne in 1347, the Black Death struck down a third of his Cairo's people.

Ironically, the young Sultan found himself to be the riches Egyptian ruler in history. As whole families were eradicated, thousands of victims died leaving their property to the young ruler. Maybe this was done in hope that their act of piety would encourage the intervention of God, or maybe it was encouraged by courtiers seeking kickbacks. Hassan decided to invest his riches on one of the most gigantic religious edifices ever seen in the entire Islamic world. This could not be complete however without the most glorious Islamic royal tomb built to grace Cairo.

He chose the site that sits across the polo ground below the sumptuous multicolored palace that his father had built in the Citadel. There he could watch its construction. Sultan Hassan imported some of the greatest builders from all over the Islamic world to help construct this monument. Even today the mosque is still located close to the Citadel. The mosque is a massive structure measuring 150 meters long and 36 meters high. Its tallest tower is 68 feet tall. Its sunken doorway, capped with a stone semi-dome carved into designs as ornate as the inside of an apple, mimicked the portals of many of the mosque in Istanbul Turkey. Chinese porcelain inspired the stone carved lotuses and hyacinths that flanked the great doors, which were burnished copper worked into a mesmerizing pattern of starbursts. Stone door frames of the interior, tired in white and black stripes, showed the influence of Muslim Spain. Twenty seven different shades of marble from all across the Middle East paved the courts and chambers and fountains inside. Yet the cohesion created a very austere aesthetic and a artistic rhythm so powerful that it could fit into the great chaos of the cemeteries.

This combination of mosque, madrasa (Islamic school), and tomb covered 10,000 square yards. It had walls of cut limestone standing 130 feet high. They were so lofty in fact that one of them collapsed before completion and was said to have crushed 200 onlookers. This was thought to be a very bad omen at the time and future events surrounding the young sultan would further enforce this perception. This single building contained five completed housing divisions providing free lodging to 400 hundred students long with a salaried staff that included three physicians, two surgeons, as well as professors, calligraphers, seven prayer leaders, 115 Koran readers, and a professional incense burner.

The dormitories, seven stories high and placed at the corners of a vast central courtyard, surmounted a ground floor incorporating kitchens and wells in addition to an arcaded market two hundred acres in size. The rents would go towards the maintaining of the mosque. Huge beautiful colossal vaults opened off the sides of the courtyard between the schools. The one facing Mecca was deeper than the others, paneled with marble design and bordered with a stucco line of lotuses swirling around Koranic inscriptions.

Uniquely, the gold and silver inlaid doors flanking the prayer niche on to the sultan's own doomed tomb chamber. Facing Mecca, the religious would worship facing Hassan's tomb. The idea was just as his subjects had prostrated themselves before him when he was alive, so they would bow their foreheads to the ground before him in his death. This vision however would not be recognized as the Sultan was murdered two years before the mosque was actually completed in 1363. Sultan Hassan made the fatal error of trying to curtail the power of both of his generals and court eunuchs. As the intrigued mounted, Hassan, now aged twenty-six, fled the Citadel but was hunted, captured, and killed. The whereabouts of his body where never found. The mosque was almost complete by that time, and was later finished by one of his functionaries named Bashir Al Gamdar.

Knowing about all this intrigue and observing the huge façade made me even more excited and eager to explore this huge monument. Its no longer necessary to purchase a ticket before entering the mosque. I began my tour by walking around the corridor between the less known mosque named Refae. This is purely an adventure in history and culture, with these two ancient mosques on either side and the huge luminous Citadel hanging at the end of the corridor. The mosque is free standing and has three facades. The fourth, located on the western side has a large commercial complex and other dependencies belonging to the foundation of Sultan Hassan. The present dome, which is not the original one, was described as bulbous, built of wood and covered with lead. The current dome is more recent and is considered a misinterpretation of the first design.

The initial design called for four towers. One was built at the portal, but it collapsed before the second was erected, and the plan to build minarets at its portal were abandoned. One of the two original towers has survived, and is the highest of medieval Cairo at 84 meters. The second tower is of a more recent vintage. The original minaret is octagonal throughout, like the minarets of other contemporary mosques. Its shaft is decorated with geometric patterns made of inlaid stone, and its top is composed of a bulb on eight columns. Its silhouette is massive compared to similar structures of the same period.

As viewed from the Citadel, the Sultan Hassan mosque has a very unusual design. The domed square of the mausoleum protrudes on three sides and is also particularly high, at over thirty meters. At its top is a projecting roof in carved stone running along the façade. Each of the facades of the mausoleum is adorned at the center by a medallion with a bull's –eye in the center and framed by interlaced bands in two colors. Tow rows of windows run along the facades. The upper ones are inserted in recesses crowed with stalactites which are in turn surmounted by shallow conchs in a similar fashion to the portals. Like the medallions, interlaced bands also decorate the conch. Once adorned with colorful mosaics, with traces still evident, the lower windows are inserted into recesses that have a stepped pyramidal profile. The mosaics are telling, indicating that the craftsman imported from Turkey, during the reign of his father, must have continued working for several decades. The southern façade has eight horizontal rows of windows, each of the two corresponding to one story cells. This gives the appearance of a modern up to date high rise building. The northern façade, with the mosque's main portal, also contains a number of windows.

The horizontal mass of the façade is given extra emphasis by its division in to thin vertical bays which end in the bold honeycomb cornice running along the top of its walls. The black basalt stone embedded in the façade is perhaps symbolic of the black stone of the Ka'ba in Mecca. The corners of the Facades are braced with finely carved columns with stalactite capitals. The twisted carved motif on the shaft of the columns are reminiscent of Byzantine culture.

As I walked down the into the main courtyard, I was overwhelmed by the main entrance of the mosque, this particular construction is a must see! This is the largest portal of any pre-modern Mosque complex in Egypt. It is located on Al-Aal's street close to the entrance of the Northern Cemetery. Once you enter into the main entrance you will find a intricately designed floor plan along with some historical information about the structure written in both Arabic and English. I decided that this would be a great time to stop, take a brake, and really take in several historical points about the building in general.

This particular type of Islamic architecture has been compared to the famous Gok mosque in Anatolia, Turkey. Many art historians debate as to whether the original craftsman who helped design the building where of Anatolian origin or at least spent significant time there before constructing this building. As previously stated, the construction of the mosque of Hassan was truly an international endeavor, extracting craftsmen from all over the world.

Other fascinating designs are the Chinese flower motifs that adorn many of the inner panels. With both Chinese lotus flowers and Chrysanthemums, these are the only known foreign examples within Islamic architecture. From my conversations with the tour guides and scholars at the American University in Cairo, there is no evidence that Chinese craftsmen worked on the mosque. However this reflects that the workers were familiar with Chinese art motifs. The 14th century was a period of considerable trade between the Islamic world and the Far East, promoted by the opening of merchant routes between the Mediterranean and East Asia. Asian silks and porcelains were very sought after in both Africa and the Middle East, surely they inspired artists in Cairo to expand their decorative repertoire with these elaborately exotic designs. Walking around the outer gate, my curiosity was pushed by finding a very narrow, uniquely carved panel with architectural designs resembling a gothic portal and a domed structure ruffled roof of Western, probably Byzantine or even Greek origin.

Another feature of this mosque was the great care that was given by the workers that lived here. Its standard that in all mosques everyone must leave their shoes behind, this was the first mosque however in which

I actually observed men using a vacuum cleaner on the carpet. What is more mind boggling however is the deep richly structured ceilings that are specially created to represent the universe and all its movements. There is a very profound and powerful sense of otherworldliness that permeates this inner sanctum.

Just after the hall, there is a inlaid marble inscription and two stone niches created with geometric designs. The shells are decorated with Islamic prayer niches. The walkway contains a very large stone bench that was used by Koran readers. Above it are medallions with inlaid geometric patterns and carved wood niches. The interior entrance hall of the mosque is quite remarkable with its dark red and brown Mamluk decorations. The dome is also impressive, built very high with rich ornamentations. A true treat for the senses are the huge lanterns that are hung throughout mosque giving it a uniquely year long festive look. From this hallway, I slowly turned to the right and started slowly walking in the dimly lit corridor with its double bended passageways. This corridor empties into the magnificent room, a handsomely designed open courtyard that sits in the heart of the building. This secret facility runs beneath the student living quarters. The walls are overwhelmingly huge and there is no visual references of modern Egypt to be found. The exterior of the building is made of stone, however the interior is of a reddish brick covered with stucco. Here the wonderful combination of solids and voids give the courtyard is souring thrust towards the sky. In the middle is a large fountain that was completed in 1362. It was built for mere decoration, but was altered and repaired, and now actually reflects the Ottoman occupation of Egypt. This fountain is covered by a wooden dome supported on marble columns. Around the base of the dome is a brand of inscriptions from the Koran. The dome of this fountain is bulbous in shape, and may in fact be a replica of the original missing mausoleum dome.

On each side of the open court yard are recesses with arched supports known as college buildings, which open into the courtyard. Each of these college buildings represent one school or law of Islam. The floor of each room is covered by carpets of different color in order to differentiate them. The walls of the both the courtyard and the college buildings are marvelously ornate, with the mysterious lamps hanging from lines looming far above. One of the primary reasons that the sultan created this space was to be able to host the teaching of all sects of Islam. Ironically however, the madrasa was not that popular for two reasons. First after Hassan was killed in 1361, therefore the complex was not completed the way in which he envisioned. Another unknown fact is that the entire building remained closed for another fifty years after his death. Perhaps because of this fact, only a few prestigious scholars actually taught here. Many more well renowned scholars chose to teach at better known Islamic schools within Cairo. Never the less, it was here within these learning halls where the Sheikh would sit on his platform and instruct his students about deeply spiritual aspects of Islamic law.

The ceilings of the inner school are very high. Behind the four college halls, the building divides into four parts representing the four sects of Sunni Islam. Inside these walls there were once students from all over the Islamic world living and studying together. Each of these learning rooms are entered by a door between the individual rooms and the learning hall. Behind each is an individual courtyard with their own fountain. Some of these rooms are larger than others, and a number of latrines are included in the living quarters. Interesting, this is the only Cairo madrasa that locates most of its sleeping quarters facing the street side, because the large rooms leave no space for windows on the courtyard side. The largest room which faces the right side is particularly worth visiting. One should note the beautifully constructed doorway to this section, with its large designs made in black and white marble. The multi colored mosaic decoration were the standard elements of doorway ornamentation during this time period.

I entered at the main eastern college hall, which was the largest of all of the college rooms and had the largest vaulted hall of the medieval Islamic world. The use of polychrome marble paneling is one of the most popular characteristic features of old Islamic decoration. The mixture of soft colors in flat rectangles contrast strikingly both with the dusty plastering of the deep relief carvings in the inscriptions. The style of the columns that flank the decorations indicates that they may have been gifts from the Crusader exploits in Palestine.

The inner mosque is so beautifully designed and organized that I could have easily spent hours blissfully observing the architecture as well enjoying the detailed art work that was so encapsulating to the eye. Here there are two windows in recesses and actually circles above the tower. Many Islamic people believe that this particular tower is a gate to Mecca, with its elegantly designed gold and copper plates and almost mystical radiance, its easy to perceive why some would have this Belief.

Situated next to the Mihrab (intricately designed flanked column) lies a beautiful marble built Minbar, (a pulpit from which the Imam stands and lectures). Here, there is a small copper door that leads down a long steep staircase. As I looked down the ornately decorated staircase, I could actually read golden verses of the Quran inscribed by ancient architects of long ago. It was here that many of the famous Imams of long ago would climb the stairs and either stand or sit while delivering some of the most insight and pertinent lecturers known throughout the entire Middle East.

I head down the stairwell and enter into another room called the Wall of Qibila. These are monumental ancient letters executed in stucco that are set against an East Asian lotus blossom background with fine and subtle designs. The tour guide instructs us that the famous Quranic verse that is quoted on the wall is from the Sura 48, which states; **"that God may forgive thee thy former and thy latter sins, and complete his blessings upon In the Name of God, the Merciful, the Compassionate. Surely, we have given thee a manifest victory"** Maybe this Sura is the quote that guides the entire community within City of the Dead!

As I left the Mosque of Sultan Hassan, I was amazed at how it still towers over all the other Mosque of Cairo. Its stern facades, with their ancient looking marbled designed windows, still somehow seem intent in warding off the black plaque that was ravishing the outside population. When I slipped off my shoes and penetrated the inner interior of the building, it was almost as if I suddenly fell under its spell. Walking down the dark corridors disoriented me in the beginning, sending me right and then left, up and down, and then down again, tantalizing my senses with hidden passages, mystery, and even other possibilities, before leading me out to a beautifully designed garden with light everywhere. Even today I had to stand humbled and amazed by the magnitude as well as the comprehension of this ancient vision of peace. Nowadays the only mummies to be seen lie safe and neatly under coffins within the

Egyptian Museum. Today plagues and large scale famines are almost unknown in modern Cairo. Never the less, the rites of the dead keep a powerful hold on all segments of society, from the humble young boy who works in a local factory up to the powerfully positioned politicians. Social and even political demonstrations rarely create a festive or huge crowed gathering in this very cynical city, but funerals consistently draw hundreds. So casual about other things, Egyptians are extremely punctual when it comes to rituals of condolence.

Chapter 9
Cultural Rebirth in the City of Dead

"For Death is but a passing phase of life, a change of dress,
a disrobing, a birth into the unborn again, a commencing
where we ended, a starting where we stop to rest, a crossroad
of eternity, a giving up of something, to possess all things.
The end of the unreal, the beginning of the real."
—Edwin Leibfreed

Although there is significant contact between residence of the City of the Dead and other Egyptians, the relationship is certainly not always genial. Most mainstream Egyptians simply tend to ignore the phenomenon that there is an entire metropolis that exist among the cemeteries. Others are simply unaware of the vast numbers living here. Many strict Muslims consider living with the dead to be haram, (a forbidden activity or sin in Islam), and often condemn the entire community of the cemeteries for this activity.

The level of discrimination that the community living here face is often overwhelming, in my short time visiting and experiencing it, I noticed how taxi drivers would refuse to take passengers whose destination is Qarafa. Many of the employers that have businesses in so called respectable areas of Cairo, are very skeptical about hiring someone who lives in this community.

Often times even the small children that are lucky enough to attend schools outside of the City of the Dead, often times feel compelled to lie about their living address in order to avoid being teased or ostracized. Many middle and upper class Egyptians will blame the residents living here for their own circumstances. Growing up in urban American, this type of mindset didn't seem that foreign to me.

Almost every where that I have traveled in the world I was able to observed how marginalized or disenfranchised groups were often blamed for the very circumstances in which they so desperately tried to get out of. As I spoke with Egyptians from different levels of society, I found that the majority deeply defined there reality by the rigid structures in which they were born into. The democratic concepts of true equality and opportunities for all seem to have very little reality in modern day Cairo. The universal ideal of human equality regardless of economic status, race, or educational background are totally foreign to the vast majority of people living in this society.

There has always been a long held perception that most of the Cemeteries residents are criminals and or social misfits. Overall the City of the Dead is a relatively safe place aside from the hordes of children who often encircle foreigners. There are some small sections of the city that have a legitimate reputation for drug trafficking. Many of the people that I interviewed pointed out how certain residents are mysteriously able to afford high end material goods in a very short time span. Some residents here have become disillusioned with their current social and economic condition and have thereby turned to crime as a way out. Often times residents of this society are seen in the same light as many of the poor inner city minorities in the west, lazy, ignorant, uncultured, and potentially violent.

With huge numbers of diverse Egyptians making there homes here, as well as growing number of foreign tourist visiting its many historical sites, the cemeteries are know longer such an attractive hideout for Cairo's most wanted criminals. Most of the remaining criminals that exist here are represented by a small number of disillusioned residence willing to indulge in the dangers of theft, prostitution, drugs, and even religious extremism in order to elevate their standing in society.

Many Egyptians argue that the real crime is the fact that so many people are forced to live in such conditions. Like many developing nations, Egypt has been unable to provide an adequate and balanced quality of life within its social and economic frame. Real failure comes from the government in its inability to provide economic security and stability to the majority of its poor citizens. Ostracized from society and marginalized from mainstream political, economic and social opportunities, cemetery residents have shown tremendous amounts of imagination and adaptability in meeting there daily challenges. Most believe that there only hope will come when the entire state, administrating bodies, as well as the simple grassroots folks get serious about creating true opportunity and transformation within their society.

The Egyptian government is attempting to confront some of the problems that challenges the lives of those living here. Many of the officials that I spoke with described a plan that will move the cemeteries out of the inner loop of Cairo into more spacious desert areas and re-house many of the residents into subsidized housing units. The majority of the locals are very skeptical about this plan which they say fails to address the much deeper problem of integrating the community into the larger social and economic tapestry of mainstream Egyptian society. The entire informal sector exist where the government refused to intervene. Only until recently has the Egyptian government attempted to help organize any informal activity. This has usually been limited to the now very popular micro-economic structures that are growing nation wide. However, attempts to control the informal sector have largely been unsuccessful because the answer to such change lies in creating conditions in which the very existence of an informal sector would be unnecessary.

There seems to be a general consensus among the world's top economist that Egypt must make a process of acquiring affordable formal housing by allowing more of its citizens access to better living conditions and other basic human amenities. There have been recent government projects which have helped implement new infrastructure such as running water, sewer pipes, electricity, and even telephones to parts of the cemeteries.

Many of the challenges facing Egypt are enormous, the number of affordable formal sector housing must be increased. The economy must be able to transform itself into a more stable foundation that is able to produce real relieve for its millions of underemployed and unemployed. In order to tackle the large issue of rural-to-urban migration, there has to be tangible changes made in this sphere in order to increase the quality of living in rural areas as to make it a more attractive and viable option for living.

The large numbers of migrants that move into the cemeteries each year are simply looking for higher wages, stable work, access to the better health care, and increased educational opportunities. These changes need to be multifaceted and span diverse industries such as communication, health care, transportation, unemployment compensation, and agriculture. As long as it is perceived that urban areas provide more opportunities and a more stable environment, migration into the City of the Dead from the country side will simply broaden, a long term act that could have dire consequences in the future.

Chapter 10
Finance in the City of the Dead:
Where's the Money?

"Let it not be death but completeness. Let love melt into memory
and pain into songs. Let the flight through the sky end in the
folding of the wings over the nest. Let the last touch of your
hands be gentle like the flower of the night. Stand still, O
beautiful end, for a moment, and say your last words in a silence.
I bow to you and hold up my lamp to light you own your way."
—Rabindranath Tagore

One of the bright spots of development that could have a tremendous impact upon the poor residence of the cemeteries is micro-finance. Micro-Finance has been recognized as a powerful development tool for poverty eradication and economic progress not only here in Egypt, but throughout the developing world in general. Like everyone else, the vast majority of residence in the City of the Dead utilize financial services all of the time. They borrow money, invest in simplistic things such as working capital loans, consumer credit, savings, insurance, pensions, and money transfer services. All these services are needed and sometimes utilized by the community here in the Cemeteries. Micro-Finance has recently been pushed to the global forefront by success of revolutionary social entrepreneur Muhammad Yunis. His founding concept of the "village bank" in Bangladesh in 1976 offers micro loans to help impoverished people attain economic self sufficiency through self-employment. This won him the Nobel peace prize in 2006. These revolutionary ideas set the stage for serious thoughts about the potential of microfinance as a way of economic transmutation.

Many of the residence that I spoke with in Qarafa rarely have sufficient access to services through the traditional financial sector. Most times they often address their needs through a variety of financial connections. In trying to understand the relationship between formal and informal finances within different areas of Cemeteries, several characteristics emerge: Firstly, it isn't uncommon for an individual to have a loan from a commercial bank, another from a private merchant, and a third from self help local groups such as Co-ops. Secondly, there was a myriad of financial networks operating in certain sections of the cemeteries, none of which had a commercial bank branch. The majority of the residence worked in adjacent towns with ample banking facilities. A large number of these community members had relatives elsewhere who often sent them remittances. The comprehensive amount of these remittances in many circumstances could be double that of the total amount of new lending done yearly by a traditional or formal bank.

Lastly, informal and formal finance here are often interwoven. A small shop owner who lends informally may have a bank loan taken out himself. A money holder who accepts informal deposits may also have a savings account with a bank. A group of women may organize a co-op (gam'iya) to collect money to pay off a loan taken by her husband from a local bank. The Women may deposit her earnings from a gam'ya into a bank account. Another huge and pervasive feature of the informal sector is the concept of pawning, which actually one of the most ancient means of providing finances. Pawn shops are pervasive throughout the City of Dead and provide instant small loans for short periods of time, assuring repayment by requiring physical collateral.

Microfinance is the distribution of loans, savings, and other prime financial services to the poor. It has been estimated that Egypt's microfinance industry currently reaches only about five percent of the more than two million potential borrowers. It has the largest number of active borrowers, and the largest outstanding loan portfolio. According to the United Nations Development Program, there is a consolidated outstanding loan portfolio of LE 600 million, serving more than 570,000 active borrows, of which 60 percent are women. This is in such stark contrast to the social dynamic of the Cemeteries. These numbers actually make Egypt not only one the leading countries of microfinance in Africa, but also within all of the Middle East!

My search for information led me to the office of Mr. Rizkallah G. Zayat, a senior project manager for microfinance with the U.S. Agency for International Development in downtown Cairo. He states that USAID's microfinance project began in earnest in 1990. The project started out providing financial resources, but has expanded into other important aspects such as training and technical assistance, which are crucial components of creating growth and long term sustainability to economically challenged areas such as the City of Dead.

Presently, USAID has assisted with the establishment of nine non-profit business associations, (only three of them located in the Cemeteries), dedicated to delivering financial and non-financial services to micro enterprises, and a private credit guarantee company to provide loan guarantees to the associations. This program has expanded tremendously since its inception. Beginning in 2006, USAID has created the Egypt Micro Enterprise Finance (EMF) activity. A expansion of its Small and Emerging Business Development Organization Project which aims to maximize access to demand driven financial services and thereby possibly improve the standard of living for the cemeteries economically active poor.

Despite these seemingly impressive projects, Mr. Zayat states, "there are a number of major obstacles facing the development of a sustainable microfinance programs in the City of the Dead. First of all there doesn't exist a microfinance institution anywhere through out Qarafa. Secondly, the range of microfinance products throughout the entire country is limited and needs to be expanded to include such things as longer term loans for fixed assets, housing loans, as well as life and health care insurance. Thirdly, the market penetration for the entire City of the Dead is estimated to be at a maximum of 0.1 percent, which means that there is still a large underserved market here. He believes that many of the small micro entrepreneurs in the cemeteries are able to produce very valuable goods, but they often don't have the means to market and distribute them.

Other problems that MFI's seem to face here are finding qualified and consistent staff members. As a large number of entry level workers here have not completed a formal education, let alone one that may require some financial training. Many qualified Cemetery residents opt for more lucrative options that exist outside of the area. Major problems also exist between senior government officials working at the top of the microfinance industry and the grassroots community here. There seems to be a lack of fundamental understanding of the entire cemetery culture on the part of the Egyptian Government.

Moreover, the majority of the microfinance organizations agreed that there is a huge gap that exist between top government decision makers and the workers on the ground. One female loan officer name Shamia commented to me that over 20% of all families living in the Cemetery are headed by women. She believes that there needs to be more done to meet the demand of unequal financial distribution between sexes within the City of the Dead. She has mentioned her happiness in working with a new program named "Bashaer El Kheir" or (Blossoms of Goodwill in Arabic). This program is specifically directed towards female headed households that are located in the most economically challenged areas of the cemeteries in order to help stimulate and expand female led income-generated activities. The program is currently implemented using group-lending methodologies. The maximum loan size is LE 1,000 Egyptian pounds per borrower within a group of five. It has been extremely successful thus far, with an outstanding loan portfolio of more than 321 women borrowers and only a one percent default rate. There is surely a deep power chasm in regards to the traditional standards of relations between men and women found here.

A walk through the Northern Cemetery immediately reveals many peddlers touting their goods. An assortment of products, mainly fruit and vegetables, chaotically displayed throughout the local market, with many women working the vegetable stands. One of these women is Halima Fayyad a divorcee with seven children. Halima was a tall, fair skinned Egyptian with sagging eyes and almost hawk like features. My interpreter and I approached her very cautiously to let her know that we were only interested in official business. Her initial response was one of wary aloofness. After mentioning the financial program and hearing that I was from the United States her demeanor grew somewhat warmer.

Halima says that she began selling vegetables nine years ago with a very simple stand which allowed her to distribute only two or three kinds. She states that both the work and competition were very tough, partly because she use to get her vegetables from a greedy supplier and had to pay for them after selling on a daily basis. She also faced constant harassment from the city council, which seemed to represent a major obstacle for many of the small independent female entrepreneurs. After a year of working semi illegally, Halima's neighbor introduced her to a young loan officer named Shaymaa Mahmood. She worked for a very reputable MFI called the El Mobadara Small Enterprise Association. She encouraged Halima to apply for a small loan. With Le200 Egyptian pounds (roughly 20 US. Dollars) taken out in 2006, Halima was able to expand her business, purchase her own vegetables, and rent a small three by five meter shop that helped to discourage harassment from the city patrol. After having such a successful run the first year, she took out a second loan. She is now repaying her third loan of LE 500 Egyptian pounds. This microfinance loan not only allowed her to continue educating her seven children, but also allowed her to save a small amount for her future. Halima goes on to state," **For the first time in my life I differentiated between profit and loss, and I have been able to increase the type and quality of my goods**".

Across the highway in what is know as the Northern Cemetery lives a Mr. Rafiq Ahmed Mohammed who was also able to secure a loan through an MFI called the Lead foundation. He is rather tall with graying hair and large bulging eyes. He mentions that he is appreciative of the help with the initial startup capital and believes that the organization could help him reach sustainability and market into other areas. He feels that in the past he was stuck in a rut and unable to expand. He often ponders how he can continue to expand and grow the small company that once gave him and his family so much hope and optimism. This is a common complaint found not only with the micro finance programs here in the City of the Dead, but also in many other developing areas throughout Egypt.

Assessing the overall picture of microfinance within the Cemeteries, it can be said that some of the primary strategies in which microfinance can improve the living conditions of its residents is by working more directly within the community, simplifying application procedures, extending credit quickly and efficiently, providing larger loans based on successful repayment, and most importantly addressing the needs of the residence themselves. Today there is a grassroots movement within Egypt for a more open, democratic, and inclusive society. The deep questions remains : Is there enough progress in all of Cairo to incorporate residence of the Cemeteries as an integral part of the larger society? Another very important aspect necessary for transformation is the psychological change needed from the community itself.

In the words of the very famous anthropologist David Graeber:

"When one carries out an ethnography, one observes what people do, and then tries to tease out the hidden symbolic, moral, or pragmatic logics that underlie their actions, one tries to get at the way people's habits and actions make sense in ways that they are not themselves completely aware of. One obvious role for a radical intellectual is to do precisely that: to look at those who are creating viable alternatives, try to figure out what might be the larger implications of what they are already doing, and then offer those ideas back, not as prescriptions, but as contributions, possibilities-as gifts."

Here lies the true challenge for us all. Is transformation ever easy? How does one balance Transformation with consistency and stability. A sometimes rare combination and in many instances a very elusive one that can't easily reconcile itself.

The new resident of the City of the Dead often copes by developing a tolerance for contradictions, a tolerance for ambiguity. They must learn to be a resident of the Cemetery, a Muslim, a Sufi, Coptic, etc, always marginalized yet fully Egyptian. They must learn to juggle cultures. The residents have a plural personality, and they seem to operate in a pluralistic mode- nothing is thrust out, the good, the bad, and the ugly, nothing rejected, nothing abandoned. Not only do the vast majority sustain these oppositions, they have a gift for turning the ambivalence into something else, something functional and tangible. That focal point or fulcrum, that juncture where this unique culture stands, is where phenomena tend to collide. It is where the possibility of uniting all that is separate occurs.

This assembly is not one where severed or separated pieces merely come together. Nor is it a balancing of opposing power. In attempting to work out a synthesis, the self has added a third element which is greater than the sum of its severed parts. That third element is a new consciousness- a mystical consciousness and though it seems to be a source of intense pain, its energy comes from a continual creative and regenerative motion that keeps breaking down the unitary traditional aspects of each new cultural dynamism and paradigm.

In closing its really important to recognize that the inequalities that are built into the culture of the cemeteries, economic, social, political and educational, are entrenched within the larger Egyptian society and are not going to change incrementally by intellectual deduction and analysis. They're going to have to transform by real specific action across a myriad of different aspects of life. This transformation will occur not only by strategies within the government of Egypt, but by a deep, suffuse, and sustained social metamorphosis within this magical place known to the world as The City of the Dead.

Glossary of Arabic Terms

Ablaq - Striped, colored masonry

Amir - Arabic: Commander a military rank.

Arabeque -Ornamental design based on vegetal forms in which leaves and stems form a reciprocal, continuous interlacing pattern.

Arquebus- An early musket

Bab- Gate or door

Bahri- A Mamluk corps originally garrisoned

Baraka- Blessing or good luck usually associated with a holy person or holy site.

Bey- Turkish word for Lord. An Ottoman rank beneath pasha.

Bir- A well

Burg- A tower

Caliph- Successor to the Prophet.

Crenellation- An indented parapet, the openings called crenelles and raised parts, merlons.

Dado- The decorated lower part of a wall.

Dar- A realm, palace, or geographic area.

Diwan- A council of state.

Duxla- The final stage in Egyptian courtship.

Falaheen- Peasant farmers

Fatha- The second stage in Egyptian courtship.

Embrasure- An opening in a parapet with slanting sides to increase the angle of a fire of a gun.

Glacis- A stone encasement to strengthen a wall or tower.

Hanouti- A person who overseas a large area of a cemetery.

Haram- Something forbidden by Islam.

Howsh- A courtyard

Imam- The spiritual leader of a mosque

Khanqah- Residential institution especially endowed for Sufis

Kufic- The earliest style of Arabic script

Liwan- Vaulted spaces surrounding the courtyard of a Madrasa.

Madrasa- Islamic theological school.

Mamluk- A military slave of Turkish origin.

Mangonel- A catapult with a long arm weighted at one end, and, at the other, a sling for throwing stones.

Mashrabiyya- Wooden lattice widows or screens with lace grill work.

Midan- A square

Mihrab- A prayer niche indicating the direction of Mecca.

Minaret- The tower from which the call to prayer is made in Islam.

Minibar- Pulpit from which the address at the Friday noon prayer is given.

Mulid- Religious fair in celebration of a saint's birthday.

Maqarnas- The stalactite-like element used in Islamic architectural decoration.

Pasha- The highest, non-royal, rank in the Ottoman Empire.

Pendentive- An inverted triangular segment used to support a dome on a square base.

Postern- A small gate.

Qasr- A palatial hall

Qarafa- Arabic word for Cemeteries

Rabat- A court

Rab- An apartment building or tenement.

Ramadan- A Muslim holy month that commemorates the revelation of the Qu'ran to the prophet Muhammad.

Sabil- A public drinking fountain.

Shaykh- A Muslim religious scholar.

Sheesha- A waterpipe used for recreational smoking in many middle eastern countries.

Shi'ite- A minority sect within Islam that believes the caliph should be a descendent of the prophet Muhammad.

Sultan- The absolute ruler of a Muslim state, theoretically appointed by Caliph to exercise his authority.

Sufi- A Muslim Mystic and ascetic.

Sunni- Relating to the majority sect of Islam which believes the caliph should be elected by the Muslim community.

Tabaqa- Barracks

Zabaleen- Garbage collectors

Zawiya- A residence of Muslim Sufis centered around a sheikh.

Ziyyarah- Visitation of a holy shrine.

Bibliography

Abdallah, Mohamed. **"Slum Areas, Slum Education."** Al-Ahram Weekly (23-29 July 1994) : 6.

Abt Associates, Dames &Moore Inc. and the General Organization for Housing, Building and Planning Research (Egypt). **"Informal Housing in Egypt,"** January 1992.

Abu-Lughod, Janet. **Cairo: 1001 Years of the City Victorious,** Princeton, NJ: Princeton University Press, 1971.

Amr. Yasser. **"Life in Fatimid Cairo."** Places in Egypt (Jan/Feb 1994): 40-45.

Behrens-Abouseif, D. **"The Citadel of Cairo:** Stages for Mamluk Ceremonial. Cairo, 1988.

Cooper, A. **Cairo in the War** (1939-1945). London, 1989

Creswell, K.A.C. **The Muslim Architecture of Egypt**, Vol.11, Ayyubids and Early Bahrite Mamluks. Oxford, 1959.

De Soto, Hernando. **The other path,** New York: Harper and Row, 1989.

El-Bahr, Shar. **"Restructuring Employment and Unemployment."** Al-Ahram weekly (7-13 May 1992) :10

Ghosh, Amitav. **In an Antique Land.** New York: Alfred Knopf, 1993.

Glasse, Cyril. **The concise Encyclopedia of Islam**. London: Stacey International,1989.

Glubb, J. **Soldiers of Fortune: The story of the Mamluks.** London, 1973

Hourani, Albert. **A History of the Arab Peoples.** London: Faber and Faber,1991.

Holt, P.M. **The Age of the Crusades**: The Near East from the Eleventh Century to 1517. London, 1986.

Irwin, R. **The Early Mamluk Sultanate** (1250-1382). London, 1986.

Lyon, M.C and Jackson, D.E.P. **Saladin: The Politics of the Holy War.** Cambridge,1982.

Lyster, William. **The Citadel of Cairo:** A History and Guide. Cairo: Palm Press, 1993.

McPherson, J.W. **The Moulids of Egypt**. Cairo, 1941.

Nicolle, D. **Armies of the Ottoman Turks** (1300-1774). London, 1983

Oman, C. A History **of the Art of War in the Middle Ages.** London, 1924.

Parker, R.& Williams, C. **Islamic Monuments in Cairo**: A practical Guide. Cairo, 1985.

Rabbat, N.O. **The Citadel of Cairo.** Geneva, 1989.

Rodenbeck, J., Yousef, H., etal. Egypt. **(Insight Guides).** Singapore: APA Publications,1988.

Soueif, Ahdaf. **In the Eye of the Sun**. London: Bloomsbury, 1992.

Tekce, B., Oldham, L., Shorter, F., A **Place to live: Families and child health in a Cairo Neighborhood.** Cairo: The American University in Cairo Press, 1994.

Toledano, E.R. **State and Society in mid-nineteenth century Egypt**. Cambridge, 1990.

Wiet, G. **Cairo: City of Art and Commerce.** Oklahoma, 1964.

Wise, T. **Armies of the Crusades.** London, 1978

World Health Organization and United Nations Environment Program. **Urban Air Pollution in the Megacities of the World**. Oxford: Blackwell, 1992.

Zanaty, F., et al. **Egypt Demographic and Health Survey 1995**. Cairo: National Population Council, 1996.